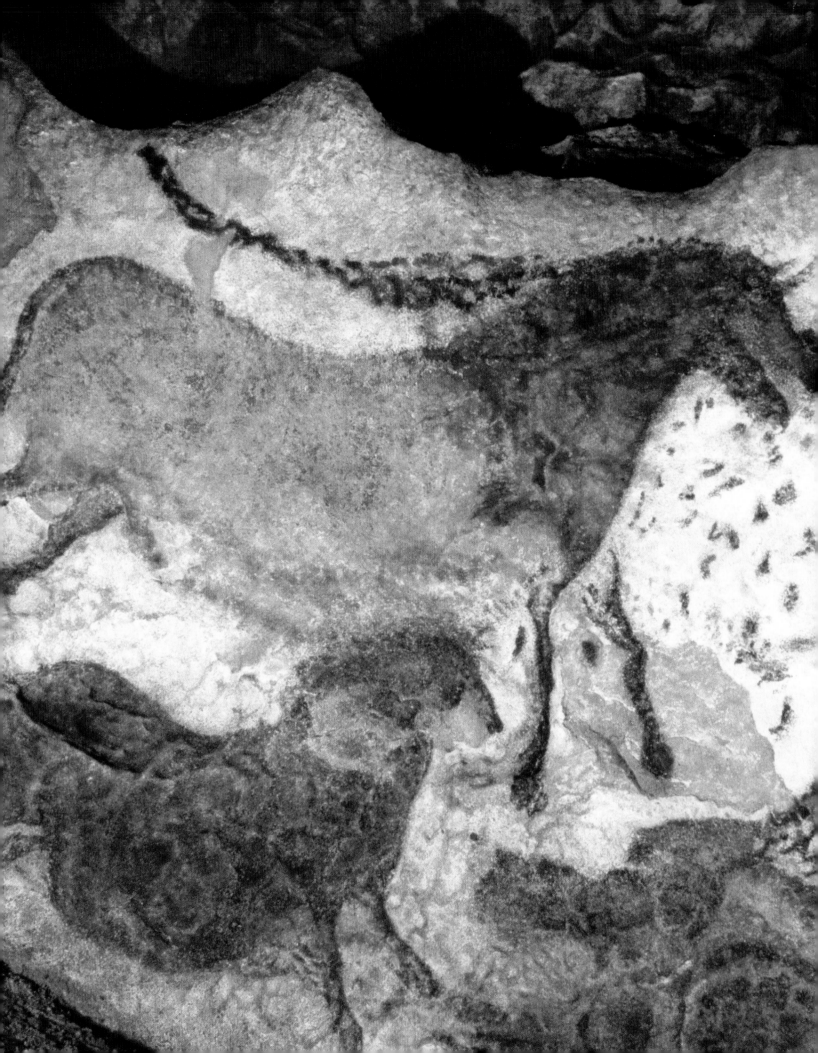

CAVALIA

A DREAM OF FREEDOM

NATIONAL LIBRARY OF CANADA CATALOGUING IN PUBLICATION

Nadeau, Jacques, 1953-

Cavalia: A Dream of Freedom
Translation of: Cavalia.

ISBN 1-897092-01-6

1. Vaulting (Horsemanship) - Pictorial works. 2. Horse ballet - Pictorial works. 3. Horses - Pictorial works. 4. Vaulting (Horsemanship).

I. Brousseau, François, 1956- . II. Martin, Valérie, 1975- . III. Title.

SF296.V37N32I3 2004   798.2'4'0222   C2004-940523-3

Legal Deposit: 2nd quarter 2004
National Library of Québec and National Library of Canada
© Éditions Fides, 2004

PHOTO AND OTHER VISUAL CREDITS
Cover: Jacques Nadeau
Interior: photographs by Jacques Nadeau with the following exceptions
Frédéric Chéhu, source Cavalia: pages 17, 18, 26-27, 33, 34 (left), 38, 42-43, 52, 53 (below), 54 (below), 85, 90 (left), 92 (left), 97, 125, 140, 143 (below, left), 149 (below, right), 150 (above, left), 151 (centre and below, left), 153 (centre, left; below, right), 154 (below, right; above, left), 155 (centre, right; above, right and left), and 159
Guy Deschênes, source Cavalia: page 1
Source Cavalia: pages 58-59 and 60 (above)
Sketches of Réginaldo Paris: pages 60 (below), 61 (above), and 62 (below)
Sketches of Mireille Vachon: pages 112, 115, and 120
Poster (detail) of Pifko: page 64 (below)

Corbis:
Page 4: Exact replica of paleolithic rock drawings; Lascaux caves II, Dordogne, France
© Pierre Vauthey/Corbis Sygma/Magma
Page 30 (below): prehistoric rock drawings of Las Manos, Patagonie, Argentina
© Fulvio Roiter/Corbis/Magma
Page 32: Noble moghul horseman © Stapleton Collection/Corbis/Magma

Art Director: Gianni Caccia

Special thanks to Laure Chazerand, of the Quebec Equestrian Federation, who has checked all the technical and historical data.

Published by arrangement with
Éditions Fides
358, boul. Lebeau
Saint-Laurent (Québec)
Canada H4N 1R5

© Éditions Fides, 2004

The publisher wishes to thank the Canada Council for the Arts, the Department of Canadian Heritage, and the Société de développement des entreprises culturelles du Québec (SODEC) for their generous support of its publishing programs. The publisher is funded by the Government of Quebec tax credit program for publishing, a program managed by the SODEC.

PRINTED IN CANADA, DECEMBER 2012

Cavalia

A Dream of Freedom

Text: François Brousseau and Valérie Martin

Translation: Waguih Khoury

Photographs: Jacques Nadeau

Extra photographs: Frédéric Chéhu

Special contribution: Raôul Duguay

Let the show begin!

Prelude to the opening scene

One hour before *Cavalia* opens, the artists are in their dressing rooms—focusing, concentrating, stretching, and applying makeup. Soon, they will put on their costumes and, in some cases, their wigs. As is often the case, they are on edge. The atmosphere contrasts with the cheerful mood that usually prevails backstage during the daytime. The magic hasn't happened yet. The possibility of a blunder hangs in the air. After all, the show features horses, and you can never totally predict a horse's reaction—especially when it's given free rein.

The crowd is gathering. People are finding their places in a grandstand especially designed so that each and every spectator can see everything—right down to the horses' hooves. They nibble their popcorn. Then they look ahead, intrigued. "Strange how the stage isn't round as you

PAGES 6-7
Dancer Julie Perron and Chucaro.

PREVIOUS PAGE
Rider Anne-Sophie Roy during a stretching session on her horse, Toby.

LEFT
A moment of relaxation for the acrobats.

might expect; it's elongated," remarks one spectator. He certainly won't be the last to notice this important detail. "Apparently they have horses running free—just like that," adds a woman next to the man. Nearby, scores of children are growing impatient. A few little tots are cuddling dolls of Templado, one of the stars of the evening—a magnificent white Lusitanian close to twenty years of age. You can almost hear the children whispering to their cuddly mascots: "What have you got in store for us, you little devil?"

Five minutes to start. While the light-hearted spectators are waiting for the curtain to rise, Dao and Famoso—Templado's friends—are restless in their stalls. They have picked a fine time to start rolling around in their straw! Just before making their entrance, they've stained their coats. Charlie Tessier and Sophie Ludvik, both grooms and assistant stables managers, roll their eyes in exasperation. How will the horses be ready in time? The stains have to go! Pulling themselves together, they give the pair a quick shower and the precious beasts are once more immaculate. "O.K., let's go!"—the show can now begin.

Lights off. The first crystalline notes of Jean-François Goyette's guitar fill the tent. On stage, enter Aramis and Pompon, two young stallions. The horses are trotting slowly, looking for toys and wooden horses scattered around the sandy arena. In the crowd, youngsters are getting worked up, exclaiming, "Horses! Horses!" Marching slowly, the entire troupe of performers, with solemn faces and wrapped in long capes, follows the young animal stars. Visibly charmed, the audience is riveted by their every move. On stage, all signs of stress have vanished. Once again, the show begins to work its magic—and so unfolds scene one of *Cavalia*!

Cavalia is an encounter between Human and Horse, an "equestrian poem" that recounts thousands of years of shared history. For two hours, sixty artists, which means a group of thirty-three horses and twenty-seven people, including eight acrobats, eleven riders, one dancer, and seven musicians, jump, sway, swing, and twirl—in essence, play on an imposing rectangular stage under a castle-like big top. But enough solemn introductions: the audience erupts into laughter. The famous little horses who open the show are chewing their pet toys with a little too much gusto! Every week these toys and dolls—key props for the captivating opening scene—land in the repair shop with missing tails or limbs. The fairy godmother who fixes them is none other than the backstage manager, whose job description includes patching up broken dolls. The horses love the taste of

"It'll be our turn soon!" All the animals are warmed up and ready to make their entrance on stage – up to two numbers in advance. Backstage, Karen Turvey, Enrique Suarez, and Arete, a magnificent Percheron, are waiting for their cue.

The artists – acrobats, riders, and vaulters – were selected for their sensitivity and human qualities as well as their technical abilities. In fact, some were chosen because they had mastered several disciplines.

Under the observant eyes of Anne Gendreau and Julie Perron, Renaud Blais is standing on stilts.

LEFT
Pierre-Luc Sylvain and Enrique Suarez are turning spirited somersaults.

ABOVE
Dancer Julie Perron is rehearsing the splits.

The show begins!
The entire troupe
is marching behind
a horse. The artists wear
long robes and present
solemn faces. The stress
and aches are forgotten!
Once again, the magic
materializes!

LEFT
Cavalia, scene one.

BELOW
Wooden figurine.

these toys—to the great despair of the team and the even greater amusement of the spectators. Life on tour is full of such surprises! What really matters is that the applause keeps coming and that the opening of the show has won over the audience. The little horses are now going back to their stables. The rest of the troupe disappears behind the curtains to change quickly for the next scene. Once more, the enchantment has begun!

From *Voltige* to *Cavalia*

Cavalia is a fabulous story of encounters, friendships, instinct, and good luck. It's a tribute to liberty—a long adventure marked by pitfalls—and a dream that is the culmination of six years of hard work. First and foremost, it's a show that is gaining momentum at a remarkable pace.

It was Normand Latourelle who originally conceived of a new approach to equestrian art that is rooted in the 21st century—binding classical techniques to a new aesthetic concept and state-of-the-art technology. The founder and artistic director of *Cavalia*, Latourelle describes below how he got the idea of putting horses front and centre in a multimedia show integrating acrobatics, equestrian performances, and spectacular imagery.

In 1998, Latourelle had just finished producing *Les Légendes Fantastiques* in Drummondville, in the heartland of the province of Quebec, a show that still enjoys success to this very day. *Les Légendes* featured a brief scene during which a horse crosses the stage through 125 actors. It was not a crucial moment in the show and the horse was only "passing through," but the director recalls, "I noticed that at that precise moment, the eyes of the fifteen hundred spectators were totally riveted on that horse and they were neglecting the rest of the action." That was when he decided to pursue his notion of putting horses on stage in a new aesthetic form.

The director jotted down a few ideas. Then he flew to France, a country renowned for equestrian games and horseback riding, intent on attending horse shows. There, Latourelle hoped to find his inspiration and also to get an accurate gauge of the progress of this art at the dawn of the 21st century. In Paris, he accidentally stumbled on the video cassette of an act featuring Estelle Delgado, Magali Delgado, and Frédéric Pignon. Magali and Frédéric are horse trainers; Latourelle did not yet realize that they were a couple in life as well as on stage. In France, the Pignon-Delgados were seen as talented but somewhat outside the mainstream. Their approach, called ethological dressage, is founded on an intimate

Templado, Fasto, and Ætes.

communication with the horse based on mutual love and understanding and, above all, on freedom. For example, in the complex Haute École numbers, Magali, always looking for a style with more lightness and balance, ignored the usual bit and bridle and simply put her horse on a thin collar. Meanwhile, Frédéric worked with only a small stick, used with restraint, all the time playing with the horses. He used neither a leading rein nor a whip. The horses were free to perform or not. Revolutionary! All this fascinated Normand Latourelle, himself a lover of freedom, one of the philosophers' favourite ideas, which he dreamed of illustrating through a stage creation. The future creator of *Cavalia* was determined to meet the Pignon-Delgado couple; he planned to ask them to work with him on his dream show. But where were they to be found?

In the south of France, in the city hall of the town where the video cassette was produced, Latourelle came across an attendant who spoke about a producer of equestrian shows. The latter, sensing the opportunity to make an interesting deal with this producer from the New World, invited Latourelle to attend his show in Nîmes, a lovely old city rooted in antiquity. Located in the French province of Gard, the city is famous for its arenas, in which Delgado and Pignon were scheduled to perform. "Actually, we weren't even at that show," recalls Frédéric Pignon with a smile. Today he is equestrian co-director, rider, and trainer in *Cavalia*. Missed opportunity? Not at all! Later the same day, undaunted and not in the least discouraged, Normand Latourelle decided to take a walk in the city. The steady rhythm of horses' hooves heralded an imposing assembly of humans and horses! He saw two silhouettes that he thought he recognized: "Hey, Magali and Frédéric, the very people I've been looking for!" were Latourelle's only words of introduction. Talk about a first meeting! The couple, surrounded by a few superb horses, were among thousands of horsemen and personalities from the international equestrian scene, present for the "Feria," an annual rendezvous of corridas and equestrian games held at the end of the summer in the old city's arenas. "That was something else! He spotted us right away among thousands of people, though he'd only seen us once, on video, with our makeup and costumes!" laughingly recalls Magali Delgado, now the equestrian co-director of *Cavalia* and the wife of Frédéric Pignon, with whom she has worked since the early '90s.

That same night, the couple performed an original number. The next day, along with Normand Latourelle, they visited the stables. To finish a splendid day and celebrate a meeting filled with promise, the trio treated themselves to a feast in a restaurant nestled under the trees on the banks of the Sorgues. "The more we talked, the more ideas we exchanged, the more we realized that this man Latourelle responded perfectly to our expectations at the time!" says Magali. And to top it off, the feeling was mutual! "He was saying what we'd been longing to hear for months," she adds.

The Pignon-Delgados had just returned from Florida, where they'd been consultants for an "equestrian dinner-show" not far from Disney World entitled *Arabian Nights*. During their spare time they had taken the opportunity to attend several performances of the Cirque du Soleil, the famous company from Montreal. "We thought to ourselves: it's

Cavalia: A story of friendships, encounters, instinct, and good luck. A tribute to freedom. A long adventure marked by pitfalls. The realization of a dream after six years of hard work!

incredible. We have to do something like that featuring horses," recalls Magali. Previously, this couple, united by a love of horses, had travelled to many European cities related to equestrian arts—Essen, Seville, Stockholm—sometimes performing before 15,000 people. They then flew to the lush Caribbean. After that, they went on to conquer the vast spaces of the United States. But they still had an unfulfilled desire: to create an original and unique show that would open new horizons.

"We felt like distancing ourselves from the classical numbers to do something else," explains Frédéric Pignon. "I had contacted several producers with the hope of creating a show with multimedia imagery—precisely in the style of *Cavalia*, before the very name was given. I'd even made sketches of the stage presentation. But no one had shown any interest. And it was too expensive as well."

Two months after their return from the United States, Latourelle (who was, incidentally, one of the very first members of the Cirque du Soleil) suggested they create *Voltige*—*Cavalia*'s predecessor. "He explained his project to us and described his ideas for the stage design," says Frédéric. "It looked a lot like what we wanted to do. And we thought: that's who we need! He's our man! After our meeting in Nîmes there was no possible doubt!" The couple, totally won over, accepted Latourelle's offer on the spot, not suspecting that it would take another four years before *Voltige* would give birth to *Cavalia*.

The Rising Fortunes of *Voltige*

After his decisive meeting in France with Delgado and Pignon, Latourelle came back to Quebec. Along with his faithful partner Érick Villeneuve, a specialist in multimedia projections, Latourelle was a special events producer for public and private enterprises. But the idea of a "new form" of equestrian show was still on his mind. He got hold of some Canadian horses and recruited acrobats and riders. He started to think about putting together a show—initially called *Voltige*—in 2001. Training began in a sandbox in Drumondville, halfway between Montreal and Quebec City. "The production was originally intended for auditoriums, not for a big top," comments director Érick Villeneuve, who at the time was just a visual designer for *Voltige*. "It was nothing like *Cavalia* as we now know it."

In the meantime, so many things still had to be settled. Two months before the premiere in Ottawa, the production team was not yet complete

Frédéric Pignon: A natural approach
to the relationship between Human and Horse.

The "Pas de deux" featuring the Delgado sisters. On the left is Magali with Dao; on the right is Estelle with Penultimo; in the middle is Julie Perron.

—they still lacked a scriptwriter, a lighting engineer, a chief electrician, and last but not least, capital! In an attempt to remedy the situation, Latourelle turned to Érick Villeneuve, who answered his call. "I then took everything on my shoulders," says Villeneuve. "I love emergencies. I like putting out fires!"

Meanwhile, though, another equestrian show came along, called *Cheval-Théâtre*. Combining theatre and equestrian performance and created by a man formerly of the Cirque du Soleil, *Cheval-Théâtre* opened in the spring of 2001. It told the tale of a young man who, to win the heart of a beautiful woman, overcomes his fear of horses. "We saw the show, Normand, Frédéric, Magali, and myself," recalls Dominique Day, communications and marketing director of the parent company, *Voltige*, soon to become *Cavalia*. "To our great relief, it was completely different from what we wanted to do with *Voltige*. So we said to ourselves, 'Let's go on with the show!'"

Back in 2001, Day, then consultant with the Cossette Communication Group, joined forces with Latourelle. In their search for financing, the associates put together a business plan to attract investors. But the question kept coming back: Why should *Voltige* succeed where *Cheval-Théâtre* had failed? The answer: *Voltige* isn't a circus; it's an entirely new form of show with a unique spirit and approach based on the relationship between human and horse—expressed through dance, acrobatics, and a highly innovative use of multimedia.

Organizing a tour was something with which Latourelle was already familiar: he had planned the first U.S. tours of the Cirque du Soleil. "We had to come up with the right way to approach investors," notes Day. "We emphasized the essential idea in *Cavalia*—the special communication with the horses. That was the true novelty that would touch people and attract audiences. We believed that very, very strongly."

One year later, the investors were convinced: the money began pouring in and the project was on its feet again. But there was no time to waste. Latourelle went to England looking for the ideal big top, one that would be elongated rather than circular. Villeneuve was with him. And it was in a London pub that Latourelle asked him to do the visuals and scenery for the future show. Érick thought it over. A few days later, he called his partner: "You're on! I'll design this production! And since I have to learn to talk 'horse,' would you be so kind as to buy me one?" No sooner said then done.

◈   ◈   ◈

The original core troupe, put together around Magali and Frédéric, was surrounded by a solid team under Érick Villeneuve—Mireille Vachon for costumes, Michel Cusson for music, Jérôme Boisvert for sound conception, Alain Lortie for lighting, Marc Labelle for scenography, and Brad Denys and Alain Gauthier for choreography.

In a few months' time, the company was set up. More than 100 employees were busy creating the show—production, programs, Web site, ticket sales on-line—and the premiere was set for September 5, 2003.

In the arena at Shawinigan, a small Quebec town where the show would have a test run, rehearsals were well underway. After a long wait, the show was quickly taking shape. The creators were learning about

equine psychology and warming up to the horses. Every element brought into play on stage had to be "approved" by those most directly concerned: the horses themselves. Trainer and equestrian co-director Frédéric Pignon was watching over things. As soon as he detected the slightest discomfort on the part of his four-legged friends, he advised the creator of the number. So as not to frighten the horses, he suggested, for example, that they lower the bass frequency of the music or move certain beams of light. The horses had to feel totally comfortable in their new environment. These subtle adjustments, done "in concert" with the horses, imbue *Cavalia* with its extraordinary aura of peace.

"The horse has become the crucial element for determining numerous details in the choreography and stage direction," notes Alain Gauthier, in charge of aerial choreography. "We built upon what the horse allowed. In this regard, our minds were completely open." Interestingly, *Cavalia* was created in part by people who, like Gauthier, had no previous knowledge of horses or equine psychology —in contrast to the Europeans, with their three millennia of equestrian history and traditions. "For us, the horse became a guiding light," adds Latourelle, "the aesthetic key to the entire show."

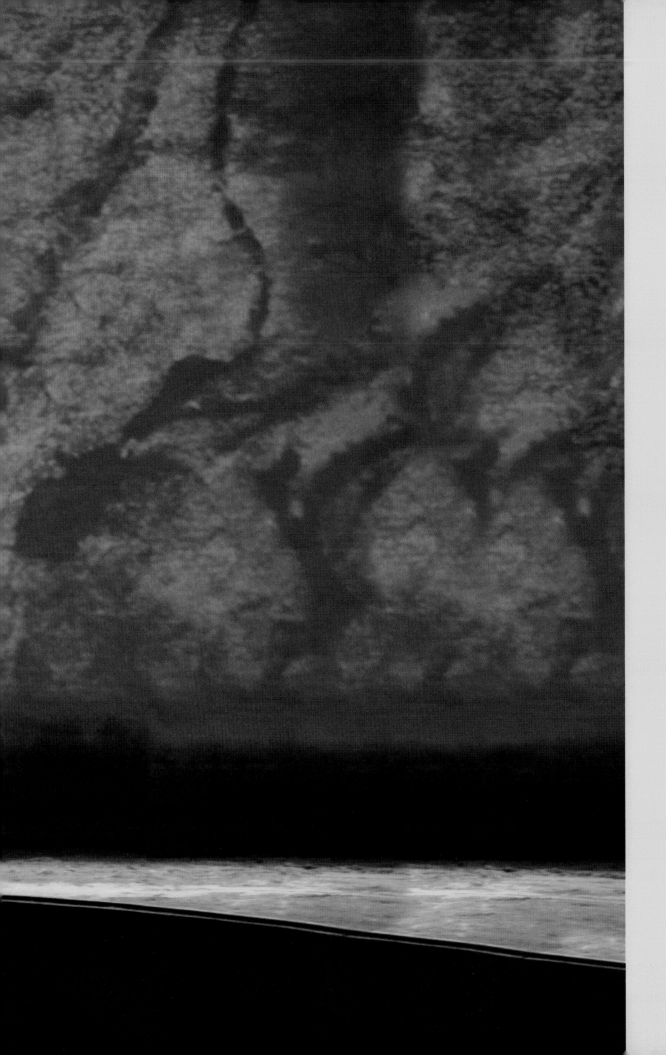

A bit of history

Of Human and Horse

Balancing tradition and innovation, the creators and artisans of *Cavalia* based their work on centuries of development of the equestrian art. The modern art of horseback riding did not come about with the domestication of the horse more than 3,500 years ago. Used as an instrument of both war and labour since antiquity, it was not until the Renaissance that "artistic" horseback riding began. This despite the fact that as early as the 4th century B.C. the Greek philosopher, historian, and military commander Xenophon had written *On the Art of Horsemanship*. Before the 16th century, horses had been ridden and subjected to a basic form of "dressage." But essentially, these rapid and agile beasts were trained to be efficient and tamed extensions of the warrior. During the Renaissance, humans began to appreciate the natural grace and charm of equines.

In Naples, Italy, in 1532, General Federico Grisone founded what is widely regarded as the first riding school. Grisone, who had read Xenophon, would create such figures as the "piaffer" and the "passage." From all corners of Europe, riders would gather at Grisone to learn the art of "riding a horse." Little by little, the continent was filled with great riders trained by the Italian school. The equestrian art then migrated to Germany, England, and France with Pluvinel, who is said to have created the first French equestrian academy in 1594.

In all the courts of Europe, horseback riding shifted from a necessity of war to a leisure activity for the nobility. Great palaces had equestrian centres close to the stables. Around 1680, one of these, the Manège de Versaille, became famous. Situated close to the castle, this school of the Roi-Soleil facilitated the refinement of the equestrian art. Later, in 1733, François Robichon de la Guérinière, who headed a Parisian riding school, developed

the theoretical basis for this art in his book *L'École de Cavalerie*, which quickly became the main reference. This marked the peak of the academic French school of riding, a style characterized by the will to show the horse's grace, lightness, and elegance. In short, the art was refined and intellectualized when the French, following the Italians, made their contribution.

◆ ◆ ◆

The second great academy of equestrian art was founded in 1729 in Vienna, Austria. The Spanish School of Vienna, named for the Lippizan stallions (originating from Iberia) that populated it, was located adjacent to the Hofburg Palace. This school would soon acquire even greater prestige than the Manège de Versailles. Not until 1814 would a second school of equestrian art be born in France—the Saumur School of Cavalry on the banks of the Loire River. It produced mainly military riding teachers.

In the 20th century, two other academies would add a Latin touch to the French and Austrian schools. In 1973, in Jerez de la Frontera, Spain, the famous horse breeder and trainer Alvaro Domecq founded the Royal School of Equestrian Art of Andalusia, at which several great ballets were created. The riders of this school would mount nothing but Andalusian horses, a breed born in that same region. Nuno Oliveira, pioneer of the Lusitanian equestrian tradition, is considered to be one of the great modern masters. In 1979, the Portuguese School of Equestrian Arts was set up by one of Oliveira's disciples. This academy trains *alter-reales*, cousins of the Lusitanian breed.

The first circus in the world, which sprung up in London in 1769, was an equestrian circus! An Englishman, Philip Astley, who had left the army at the tender age of twenty-four, was the first star of this circus with his horse, Gibraltar. In his numbers, Astley took pleasure in caricaturing the pompous military style. He would soon have followers—notably in France, with Franconi and Dejean.

In the 19th century, the equestrian circus would bring about the development of figures of the Haute École (the piaffer and the passage) and of more or less dangerous acrobatics (namely Vaulting and the famous Roman Post, which requires a standing rider to straddle two horses), as well as the "liberty" numbers.

In the 20th century, equestrian circuses perpetuated and renewed all these traditions. The Grusses in France, the Krönes in Germany, and the Schumans in Denmark enjoyed resounding public success. Later, the renewed form of "equestrian theatre" would be introduced by a troupe

ABOVE AND PREVIOUS PAGE (ABOVE)
Magali Delgado and her horse, Dao.

PREVIOUS PAGE (BELOW)
Sets from the number entitled "Dance," inspired by the Lascaux cave paintings.

The Horse: History and Mythology

HORSE: from the Latin *caballus*. The ancestor of the present *equus caballus* lived in Europe and North America more than 50 million years ago, disappearing from the latter before reappearing there around the 16th century. Horses stem from the family of the equines, as do ponies, donkeys, mules, and zebras. The Koran preaches respect and veneration for the horse, describing it as a "singular treasure" and a divine symbol. According to the Koran, Allah ordered the wind to transform itself into a creature, giving rise to the horse. Pleased, Allah declared that this creature would fly without wings and that it would bring abundance. According to another legend, one of the sons of Abraham, Ishmaël, was the first man to domesticate the horse. The earliest writings to trace the existence of a relationship between man and horse date back to 3500 B.C. They were found in pre-dynastic ancient Egypt, 500 years before the Pharaohs. In several mythologies, the horse is associated with darkness and magical powers. The Centaur, a horse with a human head and torso, is both admired and feared for its power. Pegasus, the white, winged horse of Greek mythology, restored to the equine a semblance of divinity and purity: it is a symbol of poetic inspiration and spiritual elevation.

called Zingaro—named after the horse of a man named Bartabas, who co-founded the French troupe. This new school considers the horse an actor, an equal with the other members of the group.

Zingaro's shows transport the audience to a world where songs, dances, and equestrian traditions of all cultures converge and are equally important elements of the show. The troupe lives with the horses in wagons like real members of a travelling circus. With this show, the relationship between human and horse made a giant leap forward.

At the end of the 20th century came "humanist" trainers who explored the mysteries of equine psychology so as to better communicate with the animal rather than dominate it, as is the case in military type dressage, or to "break" it, as is the case in the western tradition. Some of these trainers, such as Hunter and Parelli, were American, but there were others in Europe—Hempfling in Germany, Gentilli in Italy, as well as, of course, Frédéric Pignon in France. These practitioners of the ethological approach communicate with their horse straightforwardly and kindly, and without violence, in a very simple way. A discreet revolution is occurring. As a result, we are seeing totally ethological shows designed to fit the needs of horses. With the important contribution of Frédéric Pignon, *Cavalia* marks an important step in that direction.

Many spectators believe that Frédéric Pignon (above) coats his face with honey to attract horses. Not so! The horses, content after performing their numbers, love kissing their trainer: "Sometimes, they come and rest their nostrils on my shoulder. They simply breathe without moving. These are moments of real joy."

A few performers from *Cavalia*, in a number called "Carousel."
Originally, the Carousel was a military drill, but it has been completely
transformed here to produce a genuine equestrian ballet.

Cavalia also celebrates the global village. Artists from all corners of the world are part of the experience, such as the young French vaulter Olivier Bousseau (above), who has left his native France for the first time.

ABOVE
Acrobat Nadia Richer.

BELOW
Wardrobe assistant Cynthia Boucher.

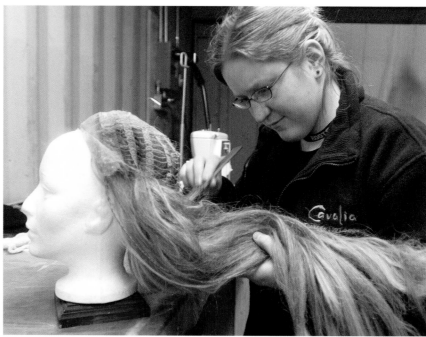

The true affection and complicity that has developed between the two- and four-legged performers is the key element that gives a unique energy to the stage performances.

Man or Horse: which of the two is enjoying himself more?

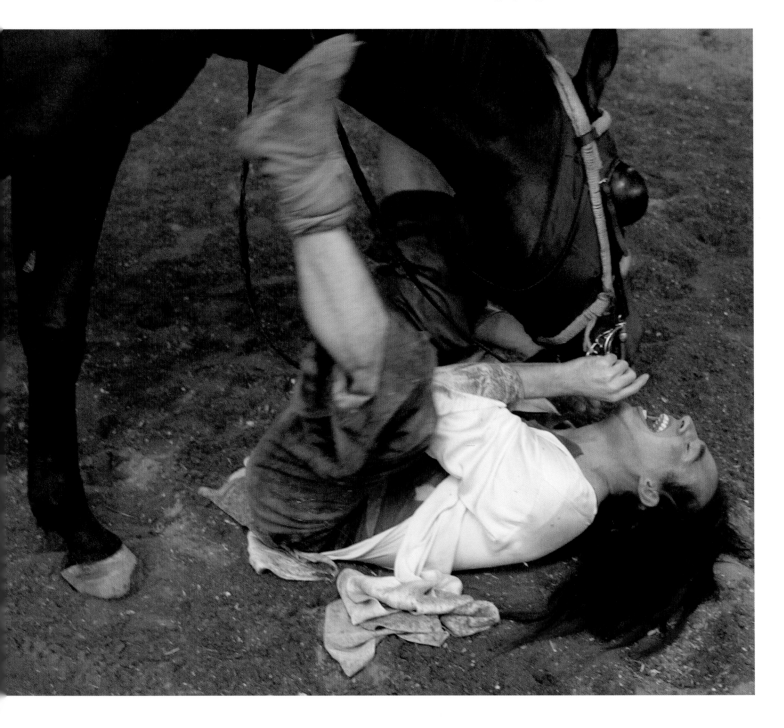

Horses love to tease and play with humans.

The people of *Cavalia* reciprocate, which produces

the most charming images.

A world of light

Together in harmony

Here's a little secret: before he created *Cavalia*, Normand Latourelle was not in the least a lover of horses! He hesitated for a long time before putting on a show that featured them. "I don't enjoy seeing animals in chains," confides Latourelle. "The sight of circus animals makes me sad." What got him interested is the notion of freedom and, in this case, the free-spiritedness of the horse—which man had taken away. But here is a paradox: thanks to the horse, man became freer. On horseback, man travelled much greater distances than he could have covered on foot. The horse literally opened up the world and its horizons for man. "The horse served as a bridge between cultures," says Raôul Duguay, singer-songwriter, writer, and poet—a longtime friend of Latourelle and also one of the inspired minds behind the original *Cavalia* project.

Humans harnessed the horse's Herculean strength to their advantage. Until the 20th century, horses accompanied soldiers into war. From primitive times to civilization, the equine was instrumental at every stage in man's struggle for evolution. But according to Latourelle, this marks another paradox: although humans did domesticate the horse, they also gave the animal the gift of freedom! Says the creator of *Cavalia*: "The horse was never really free. Indeed, the horse is a fearful animal in constant flight. Flight is his only means of defense. The horse needed man to ensure his security and provide him with food. Indeed, in his stable, the horse regains a form of liberty—the freedom to live!"

"What does the horse represent for man today?" asks Raôul Duguay, adding, "At the dawn of the twenty-first century, isn't it time for them to reconcile?"

PREVIOUS PAGE
Magali and Estelle Delgado
in the "Pas de deux."

NEXT PAGE
Frédéric Pignon with Templado,
Fasto, and Ætes.

The approach to *Cavalia* is the opposite of the relationship based on domination that has been practised by trainers for thousands of years. There is no "power struggle" with the horse. The trainer isn't forcing him to do "tricks" – his is playing with him.

All props used in *Cavalia* have received the horses' approval. From the canvas of the big top to the sand on the stage through to the smallest props – everything had to be systematically seen, sniffed, scratched, and tasted by the four-legged stars.

According to Director Érick Villeneuve, "The horse is pure and raw. On stage, he is authentic, true to himself, with his impulses, moods, and passion. He can't be forced to do what he doesn't want to do. You have to respect him and let him be! This is precisely the spirit behind the show: to offer the horse the opportunity to experience, if only for a moment, his freedom."

Cavalia's training approach is the opposite of the relationship based on the dominant/submissive method common to all trainers for centuries. Ideally, there is no power struggle between animal and trainer. The horse isn't doing "tricks." Rather, the rider and the horse are playing together. And by playing with the horse, a relationship based on equality is created. Raôul Duguay is convinced that "If humans behaved with each other the way man and beast relate in *Cavalia*, we would achieve harmony and peace, shared freedom, and wealth on Earth."

Through research that is aesthetic rather than historical, *Cavalia* tells the tale of the relationship between man and horse. It's a celebration of the beauty of both man and horse, of their natural grace, musculature, technical prowess, kindness, and charm. "It's a show about beauty that aims above all at soothing the spectator," says Érick Villeneuve.

"A moment to breathe and contemplate the beauty of the world," emphasizes Raôul Duguay. In fact, there are virtually no references to war and the military in *Cavalia*, a show that derives much more from Eros than from Thanatos.

In fact, there are a few numbers that are more "muscular," in which one can sense a certain tension between acrobats, horses, and riders. But even then, this potential violence is channelled into performance virtuosity.

Cavalia's aim is to be universal. By refraining from words or speech, the show calls upon the audience's memories and emotions, transcending the language barrier between humans. "Although in the twenty-first century the horse is not so present in our lives, we can all remember bouncing on a rocking horse," says Érick Villeneuve. "What child hasn't tried to imitate a horse, riding a broom or another such object? The image of the horse is deeply rooted in our collective imagination."

Suddenly, during the song in a number called "Libertad," the singer appears (downstage, to the side). "Her voice is pure and has a certain innocence. She doesn't sound like a pop singer. With such a voice she can make remarkable flights," says composer Michel Cusson.

PREVIOUS PAGE
Faïçal Moulid and David Pasquier in the makeup room.

RIGHT
Acrobat Pierre-Luc Sylvain and singer Marie-Soleil Dion during a number entitled "Libertad."

49

PREVIOUS PAGE
Ætes executing the Spanish walk.

ABOVE
The "Pas de deux" featuring the Delgado sisters and two beloved Lusitanos. Magali (facing front) is riding Dao; Estelle is on Penultimo.

The "Pas de deux" requires a lot of work and concentration from the horses as well as the riders. Playing on the similarity between the Delgado sisters, the "Mirror" scene requires perfect synchronization of movements.

Dancing with Horses

In several *Cavalia* numbers—for example, "The Discovery"—dancer Julie Perron swings her long blond hair in an attitude reminiscent of the great Margie Gillis, renowned for the entrancing way in which her hair complements her dance. Yet the modest Julie is only imitating the horses! In *Cavalia*, she also dances barefoot. And she's certainly the only performer to dance with a partner who, despite his 1,200 pounds, capers lightly along with her. The day after her successful audition in February 2003, the young dancer started working on her character: "A girl who embodies purity … an angelic spirit," to quote the artist's own words.

The number she appears in symbolizes the first encounter between Human and Horse. "What's truly wonderful is that this is also my own 'first encounter' with horses", she notes. "There are times when I feel that I'm one with the horse." She recalls a day when her horse was particularly in tune. Looking deep into her eyes, with his ears standing straight, he stretched his foreleg towards her. Completely stumped, she simply began to imitate him! "Later, I learned that when Chucaro is happy, he proudly displays the Spanish walk," laughs Julie.

In addition to directing Julie Perron, Brad Denys designed the choreography that takes place on the ground. A dancer and acrobat, Denys got his schooling with *O Vertigo* and *Carbone 14* before he joined Philippe Découflé, whom the French press calls the "choreographer of poetic fantasy." In 1992, Découflé choreographed the opening and closing ceremonies for the winter Olympics in Albertville. More recently, Denys and Découflé were part of the premiere of *Zumanity,* a "sexy" offshoot of Cirque du Soleil. Érick Villeneuve, who was also part of

the premiere, got Brad Denys involved in the *Cavalia* adventure. Denys then challenged himself "to make a horse dance." "I had seen Bandolero running free and doing several figures happily," recounts Denys. "I was astonished to see how well he danced." Together, Denys and Magali Delgado created the steps for the number entitled "Dance." The secret of getting this albino horse on stage? His cherished human friend Magali is there as well! But don't try to find her—she is discreetly hidden behind one of

ABOVE AND NEXT PAGE (BELOW)
Julie Perron and Magali Delgado with Dao.

RIGHT
Julie Perron.

NEXT PAGE (ABOVE)
Acrobat Nadia Richer and riders Philippe Tezenas and Frédéric Pignon during a number entitled "Fly."

ABOVE
Dancer Julie Perron and Chucaro.

BELOW
The three acrobats Mustapha and Faïçal Moulid and El Hassan Rais, in a number featuring Roman Riding.

NEXT PAGE
Pierre-Luc Sylvain, Frédéric Barrette, Anne Gendreau, and Comet.

the tent poles as she whispers encouragingly to her dear Bandolero.

The number entitled "Dance" evokes "the gathering of tribes celebrating around a fire or on the shore of a lake … it's the end of the harvest and it also honours communication," says Denys, explaining the symbolism. The number celebrates complete freedom. Magali is decked out in her loveliest Latin attire, as all performers parade in the clothing and colours of their own nations. Moroccan Mustapha Moulid joyfully sounds his *djembé*, an African drum. Other percussion instruments, such as the African *doumbeks*, Afro-Cuban *congas*, and the *surdos* and *repiniques* (drums of the Brazilian samba) are also featured. "We use percussion as a means of communication," says musician Michel Cusson, adding that the African and Latin American instruments help the players accentuate *Cavalia*'s festive rhythms.

Other choreography in *Cavalia* offers a sombre glimpse into the discipline and military relationship between man and horse. In the equestrian and poetical ballet "Carousel," the riders control the horses' walk. The themes of obedience and the horse as an instrument of war subtly begin to emerge. As Magali removes her horse's bridle and saddle during the finale of the Haute École number, several questions arise: To be or not to be free? Must we free the horse? Where does the horse's freedom begin? Where does the human's freedom end? "I give Magali's horse his freedom through the touch of a loving hand," says Julie Perron. Brad Denys adds: "The touch of the hand establishes a contact between human and horse, and offers proof that both can live together and enjoy their freedom."

Under the big top

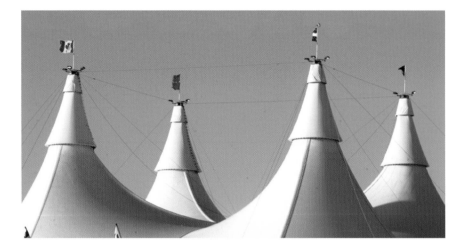

At first glance, one might think that it's a white castle. But beneath its medieval appearance, *Cavalia*'s big top, manufactured in Italy, is a spectacular feat of engineering. Some 30 metres high, the equivalent of a ten-storey building, it's quite impressive—for such a structure to resist the wind without collapsing is a considerable feat. But as well as provoking sighs of admiration and amazement, the tent was conceived for a large stage where horses can gallop at full speed. Unlike most equestrian shows around the world, *Cavalia* uses not a round stage but a very elongated and rather rectangular arena. This space is meant to accommodate horses at full gallop when it is required. To determine the maximum dimension

PREVIOUS PAGE
Closing scene.

RIGHT AND FOLLOWING PAGES
Sketches of the numbers
by Reginaldo Paris.
Digital images
of the stage scenery.

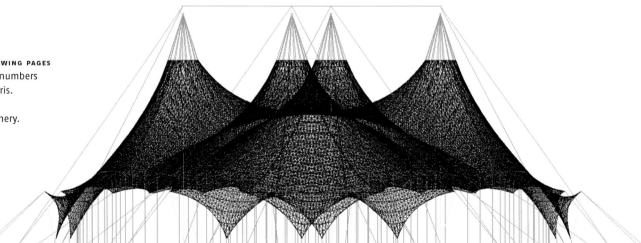

required for the stage, creator Normand Latourelle visited several equestrian events throughout the world. "I estimated that the horses need fifty metres [150 feet] to gain their full speed," he explains. "Then I added ten metres at each extremity of the stage for starting and stopping." This is why, invariably, the audience's first reaction before the show even begins is surprise at the non-traditional shape of the stage. *Cavalia*'s big top and stage really are unique!

To follow the horses in their every adventure, the spectators must obviously be seated in elevated tiers. But since the *Cavalia* team has its own way of doing everything, they decided to incline the seats at 22 degrees, which is steeper than in ordinary tents. "Each spectator will be able to see all the way down to the horses' hooves, no matter where they are seated," says Normand Latourelle. The height between rows—double that of conventional theatres—also contributes to the quality of the view. "The horse and horseman take up ten times more space than does a theatre actor," observes Marc Labelle, *Cavalia* stage designer (he has also contributed to some shows by Céline Dion and Robert Lepage). But to set up such a space requires an exceptional elevation of the tent poles; otherwise, spectators in the last rows might find themselves tangled in the canvas. Usually, the poles are as low as possible to minimize the terrible effects of the wind. This is why *Cavalia* resorts to very resistant canvas material for its tent—similar to that used on the great sailing ships—able to endure winds of 120 kilometres per hour.

Cavalia's visual design, created by Marc Labelle and then realized by Érick Villeneuve and Normand Latourelle's sketches, must project images

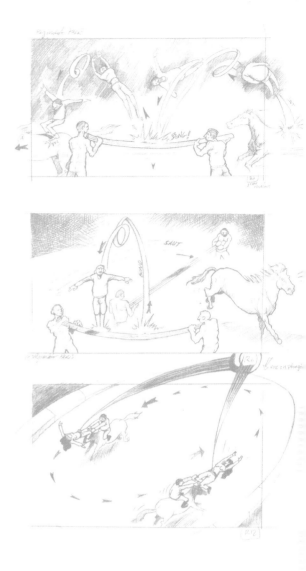

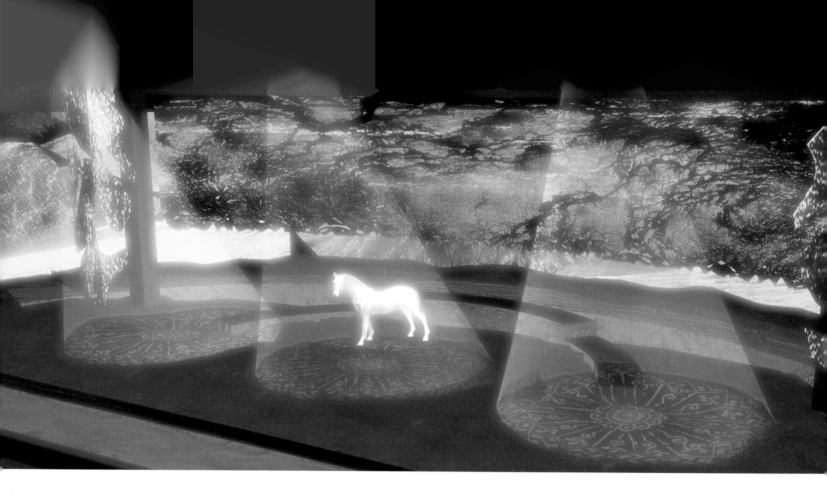

that evoke nature. Very high up in the middle of the stage, there is a mobile made of simple geometrical forms. "We can clearly see that these shapes are man-made and bound to be imperfect when they try to imitate such wonders of Nature ... as a flock of birds or the mist at sunrise or light glittering on the surface of the water. The diamond-shaped structure stimulates the unconscious that holds the images, landscapes, and experiences specific to each individual," explains the artist.

Other than the hanging structure, the imagery is made up of tulle-covered posts painted in plant colours and several black curtains that close off sections of the stage. In the back is the famous "cyclorama," a huge white curtain on which changing images are projected throughout the show, representing Earth or the horizon.

Traditionally in the theatre, the background curtain separates the stage from the wings and backstage and serves as a frame for the set. But Érick Villeneuve's team chose to use it as a projection screen. (At 60 metres, or 160 feet, its size is equivalent to two panoramic IMAX screens!) The images projected—the caves of Lascaux, a forest, Chinese sculptures, a Roman arena—constitute the "virtual" scenery of the show. These images are regularly rotated to set the tone and atmosphere for the performances. Forest imagery, for example, serves as background for a number called "Liberty 3" featuring Frédéric Pignon, suggesting space, the absence of constraints—a forest conducive to frolicking with carefree wonder. A denser forest appears in the "Carousel" number, producing a more sombre, solemn atmosphere suitable for that routine.

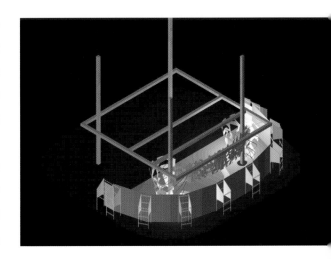

Behind the continuous projections of photos, sculptures, and paintings of the "cyclorama," there are marvels of technological prowess, thanks to Érick Villeneuve. To fill such a large curtain, as many as ten projectors are required—ten projectors that produce one perfectly integrated image, thanks this time to a powerful computer program.

The man in charge of video, Daniel Couvrette, controls a master computer that delivers "fractions" of images to ten other computers, which in turn are directed to the other projectors. "A little like a conductor distributing music sheets to each of his musicians," he explains. Thanks to these seamless projections, all the fragmented images become one, as if there was only one projector. The spectator sees only the final effect and can't detect the connections. Using a total of twenty-one seamless projections—productions that use so many projectors are very rare—this multimedia innovation did not exist five years ago. "It's a good example of how state-of-the-art technology disappears, to the benefit of the desired effect," says director and images designer Érick Villeneuve.

BELOW
Rigger François Bellemare making an adjustment.

Cavalia can be high-tech, but it's also down to earth—as with the 2,500 tons of sand of three different kinds mixed with various aggregates that make up the stage flooring. "We worked as if we were doing real landscaping," says stage designer Marc Labelle. Sand is an ideal substance for a horse to cavort in as much as it pleases.

The director didn't want to reveal immediately to spectators all the staging possibilities and dimensions that *Cavalia* offers. In the course of the action, the audience goes through a process of discovery thanks to a subtle play of curtains that hide one part or another of the stage. In the prologue to the show, the performers work on a very narrow terrain. As the show unfolds, so does the stage. The director wanted to give an impression of immensity, to make the audience dream. For the bareback numbers, and for the number entitled "Fly" for example, semi-circular metallic arches form a temporary and conventional round stage.

To light largely virtual scenery, Alain Lortie had to adapt his usual working methods. Usually, a lighting technician will outline the elements of a scene. But how to light projections on a curtain? Impossible! "We had to choose lighting effects that would complement the projections," says Lortie. "We light up a scenic element, say the upper part of the mobile structure to outline its brilliance, and then we will gently emphasize the strong moments by stressing certain performers more than others, such as acrobats or riders—being careful not to blind them, of course."

Lortie has done lighting for the musical comedies *Notre-Dame de Paris* and *Starmania* and for renowned stars such as Isabelle Boulay and Eros Ramazotti. To light up the *Cavalia* stage, the lighting designer chose a soft, natural lighting with hazy contours—avoiding sudden movements so as not to frighten the horses! "We use the technology—sound, video, and light—to have the spectator experience the emotion of the moment," concludes Érick Villeneuve. "I use technology as an emotional lever—and always in a subtle manner."

A sandy terrain is ideal for the horse to run on as it pleases.

As the show unfolds, so does the stage. The director wanted to give

an impression of immensity to make the audience dream.

A name in the making

Cavalia: an inventive name for an inventive show! Originally, the show was to be called *The Dream of Freedom*, then *Dancing with Horses* (*Voltige*), and finally, for only two weeks, *White Carousel*—the "carousel" is one of the figures performed during the show, and "white" was for the colour of the Lusitanian horses. "But the performers didn't see themselves reflected in that name," recalls Dominique Day, director of marketing for *Cavalia*.

For the premiere in September 2003, *Voltige* replaced all those names. Under that temporary title the adventure began one summer night in Shawinigan. The first performances were extremely successful—the public and media were won over immediately! The company—which kept the name *Voltige*—billed the show as Voltige presents *Voltige*. But since the troupe would soon be playing in Toronto, they had to find a name that would sound good in English—and better sum up the spirit of the show. In that language, *Voltige* didn't mean anything. "We checked, and the name *Voltige* created the wrong associations. Either people didn't understand its meaning or they made an association with voltage and electricity. They thought of a rock concert with loud music!" explains Dominique Day. But Normand Latourelle was still attached to the name. Then Graphème—a subsidiary firm of Cossette Communications that specializes in branding and graphic design—was called in. The young equestrian company wanted an exotic name that reflected the show's trademarks: beauty and peace. Ten names were submitted: *Cavalia, Cavalibra, Equi, Equestra, Libertera,* and others. None of them struck a chord or

The poster from *Cavalia* represents the relationship between Human and Horse. The artist, Pifko, drew the horse so Graphème could create an illustration based on a subtle mirror effect in which a horse's legs reflect human forms in movement.

could change Latourelle's mind. One day, Graphème presented new typography with equestrian-like lines and—voilà!—that was it. Dressed in a new typography, *Cavalia* (the first name suggested, incidentally) suddenly appeared clearer. The letter "C" was crowned with a horse's head, while the "L" became a horseshoe. The letters were shown in bright orange—and lightning struck! "There is bit of us in the name, since it has Latin roots," says Dominique Day. "The word is feminine and rounded." Yet the word—which doesn't exist in any language—has powerful and evocative nuances: *Cavalia,* as in cavalry, chivalry, cavalcade...

The poster image—a white horse with an abundant mane on a black background—is the work of Quebec artist Pifko. To symbolize the interaction between human and horse, Graphème drew a subtle mirror effect in which the horse's hooves echo the riders' feet—as if they were the shadow or the extension of the star horse, Templado. 🐎

Moroccan acrobatic trio: Faïçal Moulid,
El Hassan Rais, and Mustapha Moulid.

The use of technology – sound, video, and light – allows the spectator to experience the emotion of the moment. "I use technology as an emotional lever – and always in a subtle manner."

Director Érick Villeneuve

Renaud Blais with
a Chinese pole.

Passion on stage

In the company of horses

You have to see *Cavalia* to believe it. On the one hand, there is the irresistible charm of Frédéric Pignon. The horses literally lie at his feet, answer his every call, even give him kisses. Then there is Magali Delgado, Pignon's wife. Equally charming, she performs dressage and Haute École numbers with no harness or bridle. She uses only one thin collar, her legs, and the weight of her own body to guide the horse. To top it off, the Pignon-Delgados work only with stallions—most of them brothers or half-brothers—known for their turbulence, passion, and energy. And Lusitanians, no less—the most vigorous breed of all! The reason for this choice is simple: on stage, entire horses (male horses that haven't been neutered) display character, charm, precision, and unequalled pride, which geldings lack. In the world of equestrian shows, the free use of stallions on such a scale is unique.

PAGES 68–69
Frédéric Pignon, Magali Delgado, and their horses, Templado and Dao.

PREVIOUS PAGE
Pignon and Delgado with the stallions Templado, Fasto, and Ætes (above) and Dao (below).

RIGHT
Ætes running free.

To have such a subtle understanding of horses, this couple must have been equines in a previous life! The truth is that both their parents owned, bred, and trained horses in a respectful and kind manner. Which is what probably led Frédéric and Magali to further their research on ethological horse-training. Ethology is the science of animal behaviour in the animal's natural habitat and logically leads to a gentler, more natural approach to dressage. The couple's "great mentors"—the horses from which they have learned so much, Dao and Templado—are the real stars of *Cavalia*. During all the days and hours spent in the field, on stage, or in the stables, these creatures have instructed their teachers and guided them in their work through a continuous process based on trial and error.

"It's the horse that guides me," explains Magali Delgado. "If Dao responds when I ask him to do a step, all is well. But if he doesn't respond, then I ask myself some questions. I look for a different way to perform the movement." Communication is the key. The trainer must constantly be attentive to the animal—understand immediately when it is tired or exasperated. Dressage based on ethology requires years of observing and understanding horses. "We reach a point where we feel, non-verbally,

Magali and her "spiritual guide"
Dao, in a Haute École number:
"We have to earn their respect, otherwise
the horses will do as they please with us!"

For a moment, we offer freedom to the horse –

the freedom he has lost to man's advantage

from time immemorial.

what the horse is telling us," Magali adds. "Just seeing his state of mind when I mount, I can tell that mistakes will occur at a particular spot, or that on the contrary, everything will go smoothly." Horses are hypersensitive creatures. They can easily detect stress and the emotional state of their rider. It is therefore essential for the rider not to transmit negative impressions to the horse. And it's also important to know how to manage one's stress when saddling up, to let go of dark thoughts. In short: it is necessary to be Zen. And always, always very patient—never forgetting that a gentle horse is a well-trained horse.

Mirror in the "Pas de deux."

"**D**ao was my teacher. He guided me through a process of trial and error. The other horses will also benefit from his teachings. I doubt that I will ever find another horse as noble and generous."

Magali Delgado

ABOVE
Three friends: Frédéric Pignon, Fasto, and Guizo.

NEXT PAGE
Magali Delgado and Dao.

Communication is essential.

You must constantly listen to the horses.

Then you can sense immediately when

they are feeling tired or restless.

Ethological dressage requires years of observing

and understanding animals.

The Pignon-Delgados only work with stallions.

Lusitanians, in fact – the most vigorous of them all!

Frédéric Pignon bareback riding
the stallion Guizo.

Templado in all his splendour.

On stage, entire horses display character, charm, poise, and unequalled pride ... In the equestrian world, it is rare and unique for stallions to be used freely in this way.

All artists!

A select troupe

PREVIOUS PAGE
Roman riding number with Karen Turvey
and T-Bar.

BELOW
Hand-to-hand between acrobats
Pierre-Luc Sylvain and Frédéric Barrette.

Rather than hold auditions for *Cavalia,* Artistic Director Normand Latourelle called upon his wide network of friends. All the artists, acrobats, and riders were selected for their combination of talent, technical ability, sensitivity, and human qualities. Some were chosen because they had mastered several disciplines—such as Philippe Tezenas, from France, who is both a rider and a trick rider. The five Quebec acrobats—Anne Gendreau, Nadia Richer, Pierre-Luc Sylvain, Renaud Blais, and Frédéric Barette—most of whom are graduates of the École du Cirque de Montréal, were quite familiar with the Russian bar, Chinese pole, and bungees but had no experience with horses. For the Moroccans Faïçal Moulid and

Final scene of a number featuring bareback riding.

The stage for *Cavalia* is not round as in most equestrian shows; rather, it is rectangular and elongated. Thus the horses can gallop freely, with or without a rider. And the audience is all the more impressed.

Time for some relaxation
for horses and humans.
Vaulter Alethea Shelton
is lying comfortably across
Choice's rump; Choice
doesn't seem to be
complaining in the least.

El Hassan Rais, it was their first trip from their native land. They are the bearers of an age-old family circus tradition, including contortions, hand-to-hand, and "pyramids." Mustapha Moulid is a rider, vaulter, and musician—he can be seen, *djembé* hanging from his neck, in a number called "Dance." Also in "Dance" is young rider Olivier Bousseau, who took his first trip outside his native France to be in the show.

Like the three Moroccans, Enrique Suarez comes from a long line of horsemen and acrobats. Ricky's great-grandparents founded the Suarez Animal Circus of Guadalajara, Mexico, in 1873. In these families, most riders take their first horseback ride before taking their first steps! As for the American Karen Turvey—who worked for a long time with her brother, daredevil Tommie Turvey Jr.—she is one of ten women in the world who perform the Roman Post. Americans Erik Martonovitch and Alethea Shelton have participated as a duo in many equestrian competitions.

The team of trick riders and vaulters is completed by Estelle Delgado, Magali's sister, and Cédric Texier. An expert in dressage training, Estelle allowed herself to be tempted by bareback numbers. As for Cédric, he has mastered the art of obstacle jumping. A member of the vaulting team, Anne-Sophie Roy, is one of the few vaulters and trick

riders in Quebec. Having studied in France before joining *Cavalia*, she says she never thought that she would ply her trade so soon.

All the material used in *Cavalia* has the horses' approval. No kidding! From the tent canvas to the sand on the stage floor through to the smallest props and accessories, everything was systematically sniffed, scratched —even tasted—by the four-legged performers. This process of sensory approval through smell, touch, and sight was indispensable for making the horses feel at ease in their "work environment." As horses have an exceptional photographic memory, they recognize every object. And watch out if you try to change their environment! Case in point: one winter morning, a new heater was brought in backstage. There was immediate confusion among the quadrupeds! Panicking, they stared at the object: to flee or not to flee, that was the question! But the folks of *Cavalia* quickly took preventive measures: they now "notify" the beasts ahead of time about any change in the settings.

The "Bungee and Riders" aerial duo executed by Anne Gendreau and Nadia Richer is a good illustration of this method. "I first hung on the bungee and let the animals sniff the elastic so they knew what it was,"

BELOW
The horse Templado.

NEXT PAGE
Fasto and Ætes sharing a secret under the watchful eye of their master.

explains Richer. "We then remained suspended without moving, to let the horse get used to seeing someone in that position," points out Gendreau. And how did the acrobats adapt to the horses? "It went very well," says Alain Gauthier, artist trainer during the tour. "The acrobats were overwhelmed by the horses' affection. No one was scared; the horses were very gentle," notes Alain.

For the scenes in the numbers called "Fly" and "Bungee and Riders" —two aerial numbers with riders on the ground—the trainer, Frédéric Pignon, chose gentle, obedient horses. For the numbers requiring solo horses accompanied by riders, the trainers are hidden not far from the animals. This little set-up is essential for the security of the horses when they appear "alone" on stage. "The horse needs to feel the presence of their trainer," explains Pignon. "If they experience stress of any kind—for example, if the music scares them—I explain to them that there's no danger. Obviously, if I were to panic myself, they would panic even more. It's like being a child: if our parents are scared, so are we." The partners

BELOW (LEFT)
Acrobats Anne Gendreau and Enrique Suarez.

BELOW (RIGHT)
Anne Gendreau joins her horse, Penultimo.

The continuous and whirling pace of the show is a feast for the spectator's eyes. Each number requires a lot of work, invention, and coordination that remains unseen by the audience. Pure enchantment!

to the aerial acrobats are Penultimo and Chucaro. Between the four performers, human and animal, a real collaboration has developed. During every aerial number or performance of "Bungee and Riders," the women whisper reassuring words to their collaborators. "When I feel that he's nervous, I murmur his name and let him know that I'm here," notes Nadia. "We can actually recognize the horse's state of mind. The routine work of the acrobat, always synchronized to the second, has to be more flexible when dealing with horses. We want to stick to a plan as much as possible, but we must also adapt quickly if the horse reacts differently than expected or, worse, if there is no reaction at all."

The scene in "Bungee and Riders," in which the women are tied to two elastic bands fastened by a strap as they execute several somersaults, was created spontaneously during a rehearsal. The number requires a great deal of precision and coordination and several players: riders, horses, acrobats, and "pullers" hidden in the scaffolds. "If anything goes wrong, it means coordinating six minds. The telepathy isn't always perfectly in tune!" says Anne Gendreau, laughing. During the number, the "pullers" are in charge of raising or lowering the acrobats, and it all must look as natural as possible. "For our part, we have to control the elastic rope, which isn't very stable. We are quickly tossed from side to side," notes Anne. One day, the rope got wrapped around Nadia, literally tying her up. Quite agile, she was soon able to untangle herself and scramble up the elastic rope to the scaffolding. She stayed up there, hidden away, until the end of the show. Anne had to finish the number solo. "Both onstage and backstage we were all very worried, wondering if Nadia had hurt herself," recalls Anne.

The continuous whirling pace of the show enables the performers to camouflage the small unexpected mishaps. "So many things happen on

PREVIOUS PAGE
Fasto is performing a *cabrade* with his trainer, Frédéric Pignon.

RIGHT
Excerpt from a bareback number featuring Alethea Shelton and Choice.

The life of a vaulter has its ups and downs! They sometimes finish their number with minor scratches. The vaulters must communicate with each other rapidly. There is no starting cue; they simply know in what order they must come on stage. And beware of collisions!

stage that the audience doesn't notice the tiny flaws," notes Nadia. "In the number called 'Fly,' [*La Vida*], for instance, Anne and I play the part of fairies attached to a rope. We take the riders by the hand and accompany them. We 'fly' in circles around them. But during the first performances, Anne and I used to collide! What's funny is that the audience loved it!"

For those who don't work directly with horses, adapting to the work environment wasn't automatic. The instruments used by Frédéric Barette and Renaud Blais—the ball and the Chinese pole in the number "Dance" —don't react well to the dust and sand constantly kicked up by the performers and the horses. "Working on sand—and on uneven ground— limits our movements. As a result, the pole is less solid," explains Blais. Frédéric Barette also encountered difficulties with the sand. "To prevent slipping or falling from the 'ball' in a number bearing that name, I had to put an anti-skid product on my shoes!" he recalls.

The anecdotes are plentiful about horses in flight in the spectacular bareback numbers. In certain cases, the animals—refusing to be controlled or held back by their groom—kept threatening to collide with other horses or riders. "The number becomes chaotic at times. The horses are excited at the idea of running. There are times when we can't do anything about it—they just won't go back to their stables. But the audience loves it. They laugh like crazy," reports Karine Choquette, stables equestrian manager. The bareback and trick-riding numbers are based on teamwork and communication. "There are no cues for these numbers: we know in which order to go on stage and that's all! We are nine riders and we follow each other about five or six times each. So we have to talk to each other," explains the exuberant redhead, Anne-Sophie. The acrobats get through the number sometimes with minor scratches or burns. Alethea came close

PREVIOUS PAGE
A breathtaking number featuring Philippe Tezenas and Ben.

RIGHT
Vaulter Enrique Suarez performing the Roman Post with Eddie and Choice.

97

During the 19th century, the equestrian circus led to the development of several more or less dangerous figures, among them the famous Roman Post, in which the rider, in an upright position, rides two horses at once. Multi-talented Karen Turvey, seen here, is one of the rare women who performs the famous post, a number influenced by chariot races in Ancient Rome.

The animals in *Cavalia* are pampered. Once a week the four-legged stars are given a shampoo and conditioning for a shiny mane. Their food rations are generous. And their slightest wish is someone's command! No means are spared to motivate them: patting, offering carrots, or conversing through the language of tongue clicks!

to losing her costume once when her zipper got caught in the horse's mane. Life can be hard for a Cossack Horseman!

Three stage managers—the production's Charlie's Angels—are in charge of handling stress, tensions, and impatience. There is stables and equestrian manager Karine Choquette, backstage manager Ani Dumais, and general stage manager Julie Tardif, who oversees the well-being of the acrobats. She's the one who transmits the signals to the technical team (lighting, music, acrobatics) during the production. The other "psychologist" of the troupe is the wise artistic coordinator, Alain Gauthier. Given that performers must do repetitive movements, Gauthier sees to it that they aren't bored and helps them maintain their level of skill: "I try to stimulate them and give them enough freedom while providing them with a precise work structure. Otherwise they might take a wrong path, since they don't have an outside view of the show."

Even if the performers were familiar with horses since their early childhood, they had to adapt to the style of *Cavalia*. Director Érick Villeneuve asked them to forget the competitive aspect of riding and embrace the teamwork inherent in *Cavalia*. "For example, many were used to saluting the crowd after their number: they had their three minutes of personal glory," points out Villeneuve. "In *Cavalia*, it's more important to emphasize the horses' performance then the riders'. That's our approach. Furthermore, the performers appear several times; they

PREVIOUS PAGE AND RIGHT
Signs of affection from Stables and Equestrian Stage Manager Karine Choquette.

There are no "characters" in *Cavalia*. The performers are as natural and neutral as possible. The only stars of the show are the horses! Here Fasto and Ætes are bowing under the observant eye of Frédéric Pignon.

Dancer Julie Perron stretches before her performance.

don't have to give their all in one number." The rectangular stage, with the spectators on one side, also disoriented some artists at first. This was the case for Karen Turvey and the duo of trick riders, who were used to a conventional circular tent—performing their act with all possible angles taken into consideration. The proximity to the audience was also new for many of the performers. "It's good to be so close to the spectators. We're less then three metres away. It's very intimate. We can see them. And hear them. They can hear us too: we have to be careful about what we say!" says Karen Turvey.

And the horses have their moods as well! "They're a bit like children," adds Karen. According to Karine Choquette, it's rare that the horses refuse to go on stage. But when they seem a bit less enthusiastic, "We give them a carrot and encourage them with sounds, such as clicking our tongues."

"They know that when there are lights, music, and an audience, they can do more or less what they please. They feel freer to misbehave," says Alethea Shelton. "They are as eager to perform on stage as we are," concludes Enrique Suarez.

A team of grooms pampers the horses—feeding, washing, combing, and brushing them. Magali Delgado finds it a bit difficult to be separated from her beloved Lusitanians, who are cared for exclusively by professionals. "Usually when I come home, I enjoy seeing my horses and

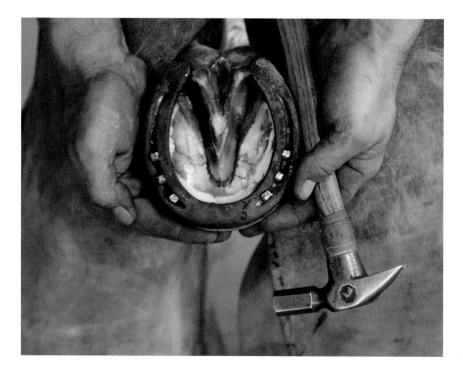

A horse being shod.

Between humans and animals, a real collaboration has developed so that each one can actually recognize the other's state of mind.

Erick Martonovich
and his horse, Comet.

relating to them differently from the way we relate on stage. But now they are in a separate stable, and we have our apartment. We're usually in constant communion with our horses, but on tour, other people are in charge of them. I can't wait to be with them again," confides Magali with a tinge of melancholy.

That said, every day all riders work with the horses. They run them outdoors if possible. "The objective is for them to stretch their muscles, alone, by themselves. If we force them, it wouldn't work. They would risk contracting their muscles rather than stretching them," explains Cédric Texier, jumping-horse trainer. He mainly takes care of "jumper" Lorenzo. Texier managed an equestrian centre for a couple of years near Shawinigan, Quebec, before joining the *Cavalia* group. According to Érick Villeneuve, Texier is a spirited clown, "a ball of fire, a meteorite," who appears in a flamboyant red wig.

PREVIOUS PAGE AND ABOVE
Frédéric Pignon with his star trio and his famous companion, Templado.

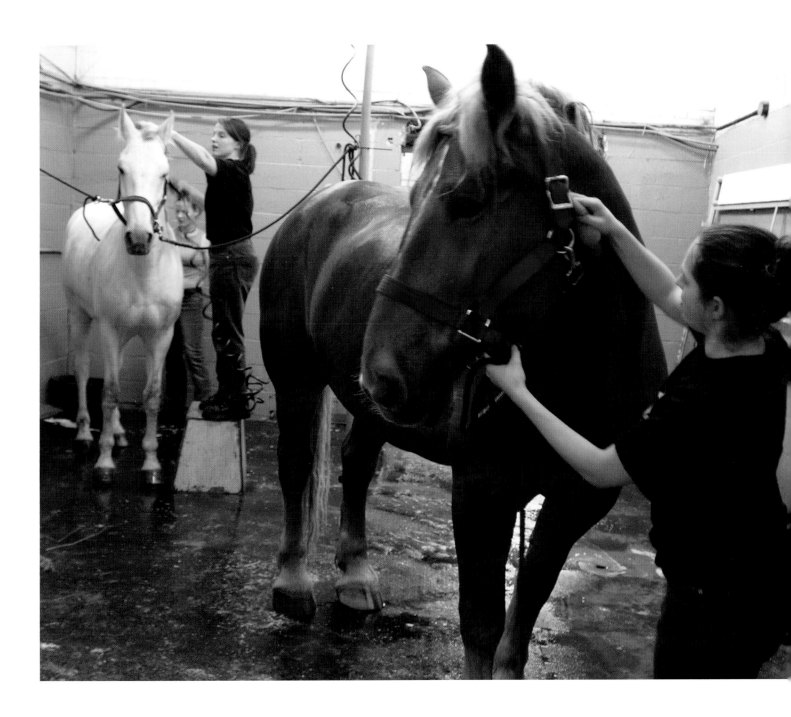

PREVIOUS PAGE
Templado quickly became the "darling" of the stalls. He is seen here with his gentle groom, Charlie Tessier.

NEXT PAGE
Grooms Sophie Ludvik and Isabelle Jomphe at work on Buddy and Penultimo.

"*Cavalia* has no specific message," says horseman and acrobat Philippe Tezenas. "It's based on the relationship between man and horse, and that's it: spectators can make up their own interpretations." For Tezenas, the most beautiful "moment of freedom" comes at the very end of the Haute École number, when he picks up a scarf from the stage floor and hands it to Magali. This short poetic intermezzo precedes the Roman Riding. "To me, that moment is like a comma in a sentence," Tezenas concludes enigmatically.

Horses are a bit like children. They know that when there are lights, music, and an audience, they can do more or less what they please.

BELOW
Joe and Toby.

NEXT PAGE
Coffee and Buddy.

Their finest array

When she received her first order for costumes from Normand Latourelle's team during the *Voltige* project—the predecessor to *Cavalia*—Mireille Vachon let her imagination run free. The professional costume designer had some wild ideas in mind: for example, she was contemplating creating nothing short of a new breed of horse—trimmed with a clipper, dyed in a thousand and one colours, and manes teased into outrageous hairdos. As for the biped performers, she would have wrapped them in psychedelic costumes and black wigs. On their skin, she would have drawn Polynesian tattoos! But the second version of *Voltige*, called *Voltige II*—soon to become *Cavalia*—wasn't going in that direction. "I realized that I had to let the horses appear natural—that was closer to the spirit of the show," recalls Mireille Vachon without regret. "You have to go with the flow, adapt to the show, come back to basics—the message. And what I'd thought up for *Voltige* at the time … well, it wasn't needed any more!"

During the first rehearsals of *Voltige II*, "There were no images, text, music, or scenario yet. It was hard, at first, for someone from the theatre," admits Vachon. But the dresser—who has nearly twenty years' experience as a costume designer (notably, she designed the costumes for *Les Légendes Fantastiques* and the *Soirée des Masques*, the Oscars for theatre in Quebec)—would soon be back on her feet. She met the artists, took their measurements, photographed them, talked with them at length, took notes—she wanted to grasp their essence. "Knowing the constraints they have to work with makes it easier to come up with garments that suit them," she says. Gradually, images took shape: "I saw vast spaces, Mongolian steppes, long hair flying in the wind." She put hairpieces on all their heads. One acrobat even had to dye her artificial hair red to match the vision of the director!

Sketches of the costumes created for Alethea
Shelton and Magali Delgado.

LEFT
"Mission accomplished," seems to say
Magali (riding her horse, Dao) backstage
after Hades (with Estelle Delgado)
has executed perfectly in the first rehearsal
of the number entitled "Carousel."

Despite a few historical references, the costume designer clearly opted for a contemporary look—clothes made of natural fabrics, dynamic ones that anyone could wear. "I didn't want the performers to look like creatures," says Vachon. She admits to a weakness for sari silk, whose colours blossom in *Cavalia* in shades of pink, blue, yellow, red, and green—it's a noble material that reflects, in her view, "a certain wisdom" and accentuates movement in the air. "Silk does part of the work. When the costume follows your movements, you save energy, the cloth leads you … it creates a certain magic," declares Vachon. Using that material as a starting point, the designer made body suits, veils, pants, and dresses for Anne, Nadia, Marie-Soleil, and the Delgado sisters. The only hitch: the fragile, precious cloth is hard to come by. The Indian community in Montreal imports saris in small quantities—one or two samples for each model of the costume. The artists don't have duplicates of their costumes. Furthermore, the horses' sweat wears out the material. Even regular maintenance isn't enough. "The costumes are not made to endure two hundred forty performances," she says. On tour, the costume makers, armed with portable sewing machines, will make new costumes. That's a lot of work ahead!

Like a *tanguero* with his partner, the rider must be one with his mount. That's why the rider's imitation suede pants match precisely the colour of the horse: brown, white, black, or red. To maximize the effect of galloping, white silk shirts were designed for the team of riders. The shirts can be worn in classic fashion, neatly tucked in, or with the flaps open, blowing in the wind: "To suggest liberty … like a deep breath," comments the costume maker. Leather vests complete the costume. "There is something solid, protective about leather, like armour. It evokes the wars in which horses had to take part," says Vachon. An interesting detail: to keep the shirts white, they were dyed with salt crystals. "We sprinkle coarse salt on the shirt and we mix it with the dye. Salt absorbs, scatters,

NEXT PAGE
Acrobat Pierre-Luc Sylvain and dancer Julie Perron in an evocative chiaroscuro.

RIGHT
The number "Carousel."

The renowned Delgado sisters live in the south of France and are proud of their Spanish origins; flamboyant costumes are therefore a must!

spreads, and hides the colour … and whitens the fabric. It also gives a texture to the shirt, as if there were feathers embedded in the fabric." As a "knight in white satin," Férdéric Pignon personifies wisdom.

To embellish the garments, the couturière made leather and metal medallions inspired by Mongolian, Aztec, and Amerindian symbols. Every jewel represents a symbol corresponding to the performer's discipline: "For example, the flying acrobats wear medallions symbolizing birds." Vachon also took into account everyone's taste in clothing. Magali, Estelle, and Frédéric lead the lives of established performers—with all the habits, including sense of style. The same goes for the two Americans, Erik and Alethea, lovers of equestrian competitions, who appear on stage with bare torso (him) or an ultrashort sweater (her). The Delgado sisters, from southern France, love the brilliance and floral detail of the Spanish costumes. In each case, explains the costume designer, they had to find innovative compromises with ingenuity and flare.

ABOVE
Vaulter Enrique Suarez performing with his Percheron Arete.

NEXT PAGE
Bareback number featuring Erik Martonovich, Pierre-Luc Sylvain, and Renaud Blais riding Belgian Comet, the biggest horse of the troupe, measuring 18 ½ hands.

RIGHT
Sketches of the costumes created for Anne-Sophie Roy and Erik Martonovich.

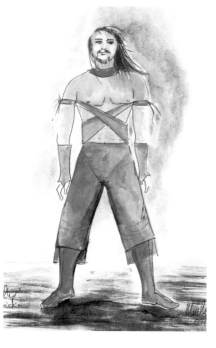

On a few notes

In the music for *Cavalia*, composed by Michel Cusson, nothing happens completely by chance. The guitar flurries of gypsy and flamenco music, the warm Latin sounds are tributes to the Lusitanian (Portuguese) people, who produced one of the most beautiful equine races in the world.

This musical influence is felt particularly in the third number, "Carousel," in the second part of the show. The scene features six riders on their Lusitanians, forming a circle while performing synchronized figures of Haute École. Like ballerinas, the horses cross their front or back legs in unison. The melody is reminiscent of Ravel's *Bolero*. "I wanted it to be like a ballet, and to evoke pride in these Latin rhythms," says Cusson, a well-known composer in Quebec whose music is omnipresent in cinema and television. Quebec film-goers are familiar with his score from the movie *Séraphin: "Un homme et son péché."* For *Cavalia*, the composer chose a subtle balance of classical and folk: "Because classical music remains universal and timeless," Cusson points out.

Horses have a strong reaction to music. Their sense of rhythm is highly developed. In time, they actually came to recognize their respective music pieces from the very first notes. They would kick impatiently, eager to start their numbers. On the other hand, they reacted very badly to dissonances and high-pitched sounds … and to rock music! Technically speaking, the music in *Cavalia* reaches a peak of 84 decibels and develops 28,000 watts of power. That's not a lot compared with the 100,000 watts of the average rock concert! Nevertheless, an observer may wonder if even those levels aren't too high for the ears of the beloved equines. But Frédéric Pignon is reassuring: "They get used to it just like any other reasonable stress."

NEXT PAGE
The musicians in their studio.
In foreground, singer Marie-Soleil Dion.
Back, from left to right:
Jean-François Goyette, guitar;
Sylvain Gagnon, conductor and keyboards;
Jean-David Lévesque (without the head),
bass; and Guillermo Simeon, cello.
Missing from the picture is Caroline Lemay.

The music accompanying the "Carousel," in which six horses execute synchronized leg movements, was inspired by Ravel's *Bolero*. "I wanted the music to produce a ballet-like atmosphere coupled with the pride of Latin rhythms."

Composer Michel Cusson

Cusson explains how he matched his musical inspirations to the visual imagery and choreography of *Cavalia*. "In the Roman Riding numbers there is no music at the beginning," notes the musician. "I gave the acrobats all the space. I start from silence. Then, gradually, without abruptness, I raise the tension and dynamics. The idea is not to give everything away at the outset. You have to hold on to your inner force for later." The seven musicians recruited for the show came from a variety of classical and contemporary backgrounds, which are quite different. The first are faithful to written scores, the latter more prone to improvisation. "Classical musicians were uncomfortable with technology such as consoles or monitors. The others were [comfortable]. It took a few months before everyone was speaking the same language," recalls Michel Therrien, chief soundman.

"It's a show where you have to be always alert and full of energy, to anticipate, plan ahead, and adapt quickly. The pace is rapid, with over two hundred scenic cues," explains Michel Cusson. Cusson decided that the musicians would perform live every night—improvising and adjusting tempo in real time is very important, as the horses don't always trot or run at exactly the same speed; their movements on stage are sometimes longer or shorter. It is the same for the acrobats: the waiting time between one jump and another is never the same. In order to blend with

ABOVE
The final scene from "Carousel."
Left to right: Karen Turvey, Enrique Suarez, Frédéric Pignon, Estelle Delgado, Olivier Bousseau, Magali Delgado.

RIGHT
An encore for the "Carousel" performance! In foreground, Olivier Bousseau.

the action, the musicians have digitized musical sequences that they can repeat, shorten, or prolong. "We stay in a 'loop' as long as the horses and acrobats are doing their numbers. On the other hand, sometimes we have to speed things up to get to the next scene … all this has an element of improvisation," indicates Sylvain Gagnon, conductor and keyboard player. During the show, Gagnon directs, detects, and organizes a series of small musical variations. "The technology also enables us to program instrumental sequences not performed by musicians on stage but that add to the orchestral arrangements," notes Cusson. All of which produces a richer sound. But make no mistake: 90 percent of the music you hear is being played by live musicians; the rest is made up of "loops"—electronic and other sound effects. "It's the icing on the cake, but very subtle!" Cusson quips.

BELOW
Julie Perron (standing) and left to right:
Philippe Tezenas, Alethea Shelton,
Faïçal Moulid, Anne-Sophie Roy,
Mustapha Moulid, and Pierre-Luc Sylvain.

NEXT PAGE
Marie-Soleil Dion surrounded by
El Hassan Rais (left), Julie Perron,
Alethea Shelton, and Anne Gendreau (sitting)
in the number entitled "Libertad."

The number entitled "Dance" (previous page) evokes the gathering

of tribes and celebration around a fire or on the shore of a lake.

All performers parade in the clothing and colours of their own

nations. Many percussions instruments are used in honour

of those diverse backgrounds.

As with all creations, certain original ideas were abandoned in the course of the project. "For instance," explains Jerôme Boisvert, sound designer, "I had first thought that it was a good idea to accentuate the gallop of horses' hooves, to add the horses' whinny—and the voice of Frédéric Pignon talking to the beasts. But in rehearsals we quickly discovered that it broke the magic. By lowering the volume, I preserved the intimacy of the moment. The final result was a hushed ambiance, soft and mysterious." The on-stage speakers are hidden in the mast towers, which are covered in curtains. The team tried as much as possible to discreetly hide the technology—an approach valued by Érick Villeneuve.

Yes, the music in *Cavalia* is discreet ... yet very present. A true "surround sound" was set up, with six speakers in the far end of the tent, hidden by the masts. "That way, people in the front seats aren't bothered by the sound, and those in the back can enjoy the same sound quality as the others," explains Boisvert. Some effects are surprising: in a rare exception to the rule of *not* amplifying the equines' sounds, microphones were set on the ground to catch the vibration of the horses' hooves. In a scene

BELOW AND NEXT PAGE
Roman Riding in a two-beat cadence: Mustapha Moulid, Faïçal Moulid, Frédéric Barette, Philippe Tezenas, Renaud Blais, Pierre-Luc Sylvain (below); Enrique Suarez, Julie Perron, and Arete (next page).

The artists in *Cavalia* sometimes laugh and play
with exuberance both on stage and off – for instance,
after the last performance in Montreal.

On stage, everyone is having fun, especially during this highly spirited moment in the number "Dance."

from the number entitled "Dance," when Penultimo emerges alone on stage, the sound of hooves is suddenly more audible.

Another requirement was to make room for the musicians and singer behind the huge curtain on which images are projected. To avoid interfering with the sound quality, they chose a curtain made of a transparent material, like mosquito netting. Behind it hides Michel Cusson's "sweetheart" – Marie-Soleil Dion, a young classical and jazz singer who graduated from the College de Sainte Thérèse, north of Montreal. "Her voice is pure and innocent. She doesn't sound like a pop singer," says Cusson. "With a voice like hers you can do remarkable things." Suddenly, during a number called "Libertad," the singer's face is gradually

BELOW
Final visual effect: the musicians' salute.

NEXT PAGE
The sound of Penultimo's hooves on the stage floor is amplified by hidden microphones.

"**P**eople think that freedom means abolishing all barriers. But it's possible to be free within a certain framework. A meadow, for example, is a limited space. But within its limits, the horse can frolic and leap about as he pleases, especially because it offers him security. "

Frédéric Pignon

revealed until we get a glimpse of her beauty from one side of the stage. Used to singing in foreign languages throughout her classical training, Marie-Soleil sings just as well in French, English, or Spanish, although she doesn't speak the language of Cervantes!

Behind the curtain, the singer and musicians play live. "It's kind of peculiar, not to be able to be close to and communicate with the audience. I'd never accompanied a show in this way," says Marie-Soleil. To compensate for this lack of feedback and to get a better sense of the audience in real time, microphones are placed inside the tent to pick up the audience's reaction, which in turn is transmitted to the musicians through headphones. "The character of the singer is that of an outsider; she symbolizes a 'witness-conscience' that suddenly appears through the curtain," says costume designer Mireille Vachon. As for Érick Villeneuve, he thinks she has the appearance of a character from a Japanese *manga*! They chose to emphasize this vaguely supernatural appearance with a punk-like hairstyle and a flamboyant costume. The singer is dressed in a long, metallic green silk sari—a very contemporary look—with a red fringe for contrast. "The colour red is like an explosion in a garment that is otherwise restrained ... I wanted to make her a costume reminiscent of whirling dervishes—a dress that could swirl and turn. But since the singer doesn't twirl, it's an effect that we are, let's say, holding back for now!" explains Mireille Vachon. Who knows? Maybe Marie-Soleil Dion will eventually be called upon to dance!

PREVIOUS PAGE
Philippe Tezenas and Nadia Richer (hidden) riding Chucaro; Enrique Suarez and Anne Gendreau riding Penultimo.

ABOVE
Nadia Richer and Philippe Tezenas riding Chucaro.

Curtain!

Cavalia: a 21st century adventure that revisits the common path of Human and Horse, plunging back into several thousand years of history to establish a new relationship based upon freedom and friendship. For all its cutting-edge technology, such as the multimedia presentation, *Cavalia* is first and foremost the product of a varied group of artists totally devoted to their art. Night after night they want to offer their audiences a magic that is constantly renewed. The whole troupe has developed a unique relationship with the horses—ensuring that every spectator is engaged in the performance while the behind-the-scenes work remains unnoticed.

Yet, all the effort is nothing compared with the immense joy of being on stage and finishing the performance with a grand flourish. As Karen Turvey says: "It's a tremendous pleasure, a powerful feeling to see all these people on their feet at the end of the show. I can still see their smiles and hear their applause. It's magic." Normand Latourelle has the final word, which reminds us of the very essence of *Cavalia:* "For those who dream of freedom, you will have it if you are confident."

"It's a tremendous pleasure, a powerful feeling to see all these people on their feet at the end of the show. I can still see their smiles and hear their applause. It's magic."

Karen Turvey

In a few words

In Search of Freedom

The scent of freedom hovers over the meadows.
In your gaze and through your fingers
you may gather the beauty of a flower and its joy
but the infinite that surrounds it
can you fit it into the flowerpot?
My freedom kicks against the paddock!

The whole planet was my enclosure.
For millenniums in wildness
I ran freely towards pastures.
Charmed by my grace you painted my image.
In your dreams that I inspired so
I was the shooting star of your freedom.

After travelling on foot for centuries
as you invented the wheel
you came to steel my swiftness.
You captured me, and brought me to my knees,
harnessed me to cart and plough.
From hard work I set you free.

You forced me to give you my life, my freedom.
You ate my flesh, drank my milk, and my blood
tanned my skin to clothe yourself.
I became your domesticated animal of choice.

In the springtime of your Humanity
you lived in a sheltered world.
I was your sacred beast.
The day you desecrated my back
I made you take the big leap
from Pre-History to History.
Do you remember still?

You have an instinct to conquer
all that serves you.
Mine is to escape
whoever would enslave me.
Never really daunted
but conditioned only for a time
to serve your whim
my freedom will forever only be on loan to you!

The first time you took away my liberty
without bridle or stirrup you mounted me
and with your knees, you governed my flying spirit
while your arrow pierced hare and deer.
I was your hunting machine,
your stilt.

In yesteryear to conquer the Earth
on my back you went to war.
Today, to gain immortality
you lust for the sky.
But Peace is the only victory that I love.
When will you conquer your own Self?

If Mind mirrors what it contemplates
do you recall that my temple
was the virgin nature?
For you to shed your ignorance
and find the will to sign alliances
I guided you to the doorways of all cultures.

As a horse of labour or combat
you cried to hurry my pace.
I obeyed both carrot and stick
together with whip and spur.
Fortunately, now I neither walk nor run
but respond to stroking and love.

Since you carry the dream of Liberty
for all the Human race with pride
I carry you also and with you I walk
towards greater alliances under new arches.
Let Love be your only Glory
and the reins of Power will be yours.

I used to be but a servile and useful animal.
You shaped me into a work of art.
Today my greatest use
is to please you and that is easy for me.
Since I feel free and secure
I no longer want to flee but come towards you.
You are my most noble conquest, my joy.

Raôul Duguay

Carousel: The Carousel is equestrian choreography with music done in synchronism. It dates back to the 17th century. It is said that Louis XIV of France was especially fond of it. Carousels were originally performed in the riding schools adjoining royal palaces.

Dressage: Dressage is a training method intended to make a horse easier and more agreeable to ride. It is also an equestrian discipline. The trainer teaches the horse movements and figures in a progressive and regular manner. The training of a horse can be compared to the education of a child. For its dressage numbers, Cavalia chose Lusitanian horses ridden by the star sisters Magali and Estelle Delgado, who are the designated riders for all Haute École numbers. These horses are known for their strength and courage. Renowned as well for their majestic poise and sense of showmanship, they have performed **Haute École** figures for many centuries.

Haute École (also called High School): The teachings of the Haute École consist of a series of exercises that are taught only after horses master the figures of advanced **dressage** (change of leg, shoulder-in, to collect, etc.). This ultimate step in the course of the training culminates in such movements as **piaffer**, **passage**, **levade**, rearing (**pesade**), and pirouette at the canter. The figures of the Haute École were inspired by European equestrian traditions.

Liberty: As their name suggests, the liberty numbers are ones in which the horse is left free. This means that the horse is "nude," with neither saddle, bit, nor any type of harness. The rider only carries a small stick to occasionally guide the horse's movements.

Equestrian Terms

Cabrade

Carousel

Haute École

Spanish walk

Pas de deux: This number involves two riders performing choreography. Thanks to their physical similarities, the Delgado sisters have created a "mirror" Pas de deux. During this dance, each seems to be the reflection of the other. It's a highly technical and complex number. The Lusitanians trot in place at the same cadence, perform synchronized movements (**passage**) and stretch their foreleg (**Spanish walk**). The Pas de deux was practised at the Saumur School as early as the beginning of the 19th century.

Spanish walk: Four-beat rhythmic step in which the horse extends his forelegs, holds them high, then brings them down to the ground straight-kneed.

Passage: Perfect and slow ballet-like trot in which the horse pauses before majestically bringing his foreleg to the ground. It's one of the key figures of the "Carousel" number.

Pesade (or rearing): Figure in which the horse rears on his hind legs with his forelegs lifted in the air. The Lusitanians love performing this figure in the "Liberty" number. They form an angle of over 45 degrees from the ground. The **pesade** are natural

positions for the horse, mainly when he is running away.

Piaffer: A passage in place and in a high action in which the horse brings his forelegs to the ground alternately, going neither forward nor backward.

Roman Post: The Roman Post is a trick-riding figure very popular in the circus, in which the rider stands on the rumps of two horses while holding the reins in each hand. The harnessing is held with long reins, with or without a halter – Vaulter Karen Truvey of *Cavalia* doesn't use one – and is the product of an ancient Hungarian peasant tradition. The Sczikos horsemen, who guarded herds of cattle and flocks of sheep, used to perform this figure. On today's stage, the Roman Post is practised by imaginative vaulters who run the risk of taking some astonishing tumbles. Using two or more horses and various speeds, the Roman Post showcases both riders and horses.

Obstacle jumping: Horses were originally trained to perform these figures in times of war. They had to be prepared to overcome all sorts of obstacles on the roads. The first obstacle jumping competition took place in Dublin, Ireland, in 1865. This discipline was

Piaffer

Roman Post

later officially recognized as an equestrian sport at the 1912 Olympic Games in Stockholm. Historically, Europe has always been a champion in show jumping. In *Cavalia*, Lorenzo – an American Warmblood – is the only horse that performs obstacle jumps.

Vaulting: Vaulting is a traditional equestrian sport that consists of gymnastic and acrobatic routines and figures (scissor, somersault, windmill, and several others) performed on the horse's rump. Vaulting started in the circus and as a stretching exercise in military training. It can be done as a solo, a duo, or a trio. The figures are performed while the horse gallops along the sides of a circular arena. The rhythm is rapid. Any sudden change in the horse's speed can cause the rider to fall. The horse wears a strap with two handles, enabling the rider to mount the horse or to hold on to it while in "flight." The rider may also use the strap and handles to complete a scissor. The horse used in trick-riding must be robust and have a very wide rump to enable the rider to stand or jump on the carpet placed on the rump to protect the horse. *Cavalia* uses draft horses, namely big Belgians and Percherons (originally from Le Perche, near Normandy in France). These horses hold the record for size and strength and are still used for this reason on farms. In the past, they used to accompany horsemen to war.

Cossack Hang: Spectacular and breathtaking is the Cossack Hang! It consists of releasing a horse and its rider at full speed in a straight line. The rider holds on to the handles and straps of a Cossack saddle (western or American saddles are also used in *Cavalia* for this very popular number, which is performed at the end of the show). The rider can then perform daring acrobatics: let

Trick riding

his head hang on one side of the horse, pick up objects on the ground, remain hidden and suspended behind his horse in full movement, perform a "scissor." These daredevil figures originate with the Cossacks of southern Russia – a people made up of freed peasants and soldiers who guarded the borders of Russia and Poland against Turkish invasions. To hide from the enemy, the Cossack horsemen hid on the sides or underneath their horses! For the Cossack figures, *Cavalia* features Lusitanians and quarter-horses. The American quarter-horse is very muscular, docile, and tolerant. He is known for his speed in short-distance runs – including the quarter-mile run, from which the animal takes his name.

Bareback riding

Ætes ◆ Spanish-frison, white stallion, age 13

Aramis ◆ Arabian, black foal, 10 months

Arete ◆ Percheron, grey gelding, age 7

Bandit ◆ Quarter-horse, bay gelding, age 5

Bandolero ◆ Lusitano, albino stallion, age 13

Ben ◆ Quarter-horse, dark bay gelding, age 5

Buddy ◆ Belgian, chestnut gelding, age 6

Choice ◆ Quarter-horse, dark bay gelding, age 17

Chucaro ◆ Lusitano, grey stallion, age 13

Coffee ◆ Percheron, black gelding, age 6

Comet ◆ Belgian, blond chestnut gelding, age 6

Dao ◆ Lusitano, white stallion, age 12

Eddy ◆ Quarter-horse, black gelding, age 17
(background: Choice)

Choice, Tobby, and Joe (hidden).

Edros ◆ Lusitano, grey stallion, age 11

Famoso ◆ Lusitano, grey stallion, age 10

Fasto ◆ Lusitano, white stallion, age 10

Gracil ◆ Lusitano, buckskin stallion, age 9

Bandit in the process of being shod.

Guizo ◆ Lusitano, black stallion, age 9

Hades ◆ Lusitano, grey stallion, age 8

Hollywood ◆ Quarter-horse, chestnut gelding, age 7

Joe ◆ Quarter-horse, chestnut gelding, age 7

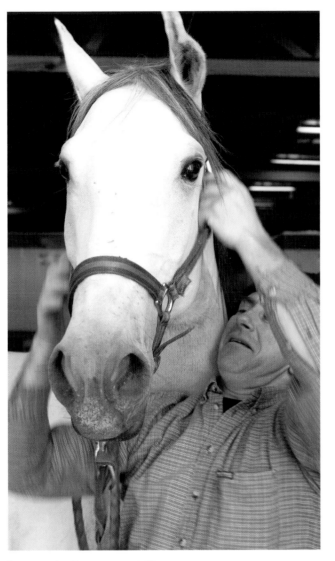

Iman ◆ Lusitano, grey stallion, age 7

Kiwi ◆ Quarter-horse, bay gelding, age 4

Lorenzo ◆ Warmblood, dark bay gelding, age 7

Mandarin ◆ Lusitano, buckskin stallion, age 4

Penultimo ◆ Spanish, white gelding, age 12

Joe taking a quiet moment.

Pico ◆ Appalloosa, gelding, age 4

Pompon ◆ Quarter-horse, palomino, 8 months

Popeye ◆ Quarter-horse, bay stallion, age 15

T-Bar ◆ Quarter-horse, copper chestnut stallion, age 10

Templado ◆ Lusitano, white stallion, age 17

Tobby ◆ Quarter-horse, copper chestnut gelding, age 5

Zazabelou ◆ Lusitano, buckskin stallion, age 7

Wooden figurine used during the performance.

Normand Latourelle, Dominique Day, Frédéric Pignon, and Magali Delgado

ALAIN LORTIE
Lighting designer

MIREILLE VACHON
Costume designer

JÉRÔME BOISVERT
Sound designer

MARC LABELLE
Scenic designer

BRAD DENYS
Choreographer

ÉRICK VILLENEUVE
Director and visual designer

MICHEL CUSSON
Music composer

Creative artists

NORMAND LATOURELLE • Artistic director
ÉRICK VILLENEUVE • Director and visual designer
FRÉDÉRIC PIGNON • Equestrian director
MAGALI DELGADO • Equestrian director
MICHEL CUSSON • Music composer
ALAIN LORTIE • Lighting designer
MIREILLE VACHON • Costume designer
MARC LABELLE • Scenic designer
BRAD DENYS • Choreographer
ALAIN GAUTHIER • Choreographer and artistic coordinator on tour
JÉRÔME BOISVERT • Sound designer
SORAYA BENITEZ AND NORMAND LATOURELLE • Lyrics
LOUIS CÔTÉ • Assistant to the director
VALÉRIE GAREAU • Assistant to the artistic director

Artists (in alphabetical order)

FRÉDÉRIC BARRETTE • Acrobat (Russian bar porter, ball, trampoline, hand-to-hand)
RENAUD BLAIS • Acrobat (Russian bar porter, trampoline, Chinese pole)
OLIVIER BOUSSEAU • Rider, roman rider, trick rider, and assistant horse trainer
MAGALI DELGADO • Equestrian director, dressage rider, and dressage horse trainer
ESTELLE DELGADO • Dressage rider, trick rider, and dressage horse trainer
ANNE GENDREAU • Acrobat (bungee, aerial pas de deux)
DOSBERGEN KOZUGULOV • Vaulter
ERIK MARTONOVICH • Vaulter
FAÏÇAL MOULID • Acrobat (contortion, tumbling, trampoline)
MUSTAPHA MOULID • Acrobat (tumbling, trampoline), vaulter
JULIE PERRON • Dancer
FRÉDÉRIC PIGNON • Equestrian director, liberty horse trainer, and rider
EL HASSAN RAIS • Acrobat (tumbling, contortion, trampoline)
NADIA RICHER • Acrobat (bungee, aerial pas de deux)
ANNE-SOPHIE ROY • Vaulter
ALETHEA SHELTON • Vaulter
ENRIQUE SUAREZ • Vaulter, rider, and draft horse trainer
PIERRE-LUC SYLVAIN • Acrobat (Russian bar flyer, straps, tumbling, trampoline, hand-to-hand)
CÉDRIC TEXIER • Jumper, jumping horse trainer
PHILIPPE TEZENAS DU MONTCEL • Rider
KAREN TURVEY • Roman rider, trick rider, rider, and quarter-horse trainer

Musicians

MARIE-SOLEIL DION • Singer
SYLVAIN GAGNON • Conductor and keyboards
JEAN-DAVID LÉVESQUE • Bass, percussions, and turn tables
ÉRIC BOUDREAULT • Drums and percussion
JEAN-FRANÇOIS GOYETTE • Guitar
CAROLINE LEMAY • Oboe
GUILLERMO SIMÉON • Cello

Stables

KARINE CHOQUETTE • Stables manager and equestrian stage manager
ANDREA K. E. SHEPLEY • Veterinarian technician
MARIE-CLAUDE LOISELLE • Assistant to the veterinarian technician
CHARLIE TESSIER • Groom
JONATHAN GAUCHER • Groom
SOPHIE LUDVIK • Groom
ISABELLE JOMPHE • Groom
JEAN SAUVAGEAU • Groom
BENOIT GAUVIN • Groom
ÉDITH FORTIN • Groom
PASCAL HENRY • Groom
JÉRÔME PARK • Blacksmith

Production

PATRICK LOUBERT • Tour director
JOHANNE THIBODEAU • Assistant to the tour director
CHRISTINE B. PICARD • On-tour services manager
MARTIN PARENT • Computer coordinator
GUY BELLEMARRE • Computer technician
JULIE TARDIF • Stage manager
ANI DUMAS • Assistant to the stage manager
MADELEINE BÉLAIR • Head of wardrobe
CYNTHIA BOUCHER • Wardrobe assistant
LOUISE BOURRET • Assistant to the artistic manager
JAMES A. RICHARDSON • Technical director
MICHEL THERRIEN • Chief sound operator and technical director
PIERRE SANSCHAGRIN • Sound operator assistant
SERGE BELLEAU • Head carpenter
FRÉDÉRIK VALLIÈRES • Carpenter
ISABELLE ARCHAMBAULT • Carpenter
MARCO POPPY ALLARD • Lighting board operator
SYLVAIN RED RACINE • Electrician manager
SÉBASTIEN GAGNON • Follow spots operator
DANIEL COUVRETTE • Video manager
MARC LABRANCHE • Head rigger
FRANÇOIS BELLEMARE • Rigger
MATHIEU GUÉRIN • Site electrician
JEAN-PIERRE DERASPE • Electrician assistant
ÉTIENNE LABRECQUE • Site technician
NICOLAS PAULETTE • Logistics director
HÉLÈNE CARON • Logistics assistant
STÉPHANE BIRTZ • Site coordinator
GUY ROSSIGNOL • Big top foreman
MARC LACROIX • Big top foreman

Pre-production

SERGE GAUTHIER • Production director
LOUIS CÔTÉ • Stage manager
NICOLAS PAULETTE • Logistics director
LUC VAUGEOIS • Development coordinator
JEAN-GUY LACROIX • Assistant to the Logistics director
JANICK WOLPUTT • Tent master
SUZANNE GOSSELIN • Production assistant
DIANE NOËL • Production assistant

STÉPHANE PILON • Tent master assistant
ISABELLE VILLENEUVE • Acting coach
ANDRÉ ST-JEAN • Acrobatic coach
DEBRA BROWN • Choreographer adviser
JOHANNE VÉZINA • Assistant to the set designer
GEORGES RINGUETTE • Set design assistant
DANIELLE BROSSEAU • Costume designer assistant
MARYSE GAUTHIER • Patternmaker
NATASHA MASSICOTTE • Seamstress
ISABELLE GRANIER • Seamstress
JACKIE MORIN • Property person
DÉLINE PÉTRONE • Dyer
PAUL ROSE • Patternmaker
HÉLÈNE TÉTREAULT • Wardrobe property person
GISÈLE BÉLAND • Equestrian property person
CHRISTIANNE THÉBERGE • Patternmaker
MIKIE HAMILTON • Mitho makeup designer
MÉLANIE GUIMONT • Makeup assistant
JESSICA MANZO • Makeup assistant
JOHANNE PILLETTE • Makeup assistant
MANON DUGUAY • Research assistant
NICOLAS D'OSTIE • Video editor
LOUIS-PIERRE MORIN • Graphic designer
PIERRE-ALEXIS TREMBLAY • Graphic designer

Public Services

CATHERINE LOUBIER • Public services director
JÉRÔME DROUIN • Assistant to the public services director
MATHIEU LATOURELLE • Merchandising coordinator
GUY TREMBLAY • Head usher
JOSÉE LAUZIER • Concession coordinator
MARIE-CLAUDE GEOFFRION • Coordinator, Cavalia rendez-vous package
MICHELLE LAREAU • Cavalia rendez-vous welcome agent

Ticket Office

CAROLE VERMETTE • Ticket office director
FRANÇOIS BERGERON • Ticket office supervisor – Montreal
JUSTIN ROUSSEAU • Ticket office supervisor – on tour
NAOMI ADLER • Assistant to the supervisor
JULIE MONGRAIN • Ticket agent

Artisans

On tour

Marketing and Communications

DOMINIQUE DAY · Marketing and communications director

MARTIN ROY · Publicist

FABIENNE THOMAS · Communication agent

FRANÇOISE CABANA · Assistant to the marketing and communications director

SÉBASTIEN POIRIER · Graphic designer

GRAPHÈME · Branding and graphic design

Administration

NORMAND LATOURELLE · President and general manager

SERGE GAUTHIER · Operation director

STÉPHANE MICHAUD · Finance and administration director

DAVID PARR · Market development director

CAROLE VERMETTE · Assistant to operation director

ROSARIA PERSECHINI · Assistant to the president and general manager

JACYNTHE MARCOTTE · Assistant to the finance and administration director

ANNIE MARTEL · Corporate chief accountant

GUY SAVARD · Tour accountant

MONIQUE DUMONT · Tour accounting assistant

BRUNO OSTIGUY · Financial analyst

DIANE CLOUTIER · Payroll

Board of directors

NORMAND LATOURELLE · President

DOMINIQUE DAY · Vice-president

PHILIPPE-DENIS RICHARD · Secretary-treasurer

FRANÇOIS DUFFAR · Director

WEB SITE:

www.cavalia.net

Head office

Artistic management

The musicians

Stables

Marketing and communications

The artists

Public services

Three snapshots of the production team

Contents